HUNTING
BIG MULE DEER

HOW TO TAKE THE
BEST BUCK
OF YOUR LIFE

Robby Denning

HUNTING BIG MULE DEER:
HOW TO TAKE THE BEST BUCK OF YOUR LIFE

Author photos copyright Robby Denning,
robby@rokslide.com
Other photos courtesy of 123rf.com
and
Rod Sinclair at sinclairimageryinc.com
Taxidermy by Denning Taxidermy, Ammon, Idaho
Cowboy art ©2015 Stacy Beazer-Rogers
stacybeazerrogers.com

The "Brokenheart Buck" story was first published by
Christensen's *Hunting Illustrated* Magazine.
Editing and book design by AnderssonPublishing.com

ISBN-13: 978-0-692-45795-5
ISBN-10: 069245795X

Printed in the United States of America
Published by WeScout4u.com

DEDICATION

To my father, Doug,
Thanks Dad, for always being there.
I promise to do the same for your grandkids.

12/13/2018

Darryl & Linda

Merry Christmas and Happy Holidays to you and Yours.

A short note of appreciation with regard to some great outings, fishing and hunting trips.
Your sense of humor, expertise and professionalism certainly made those trips both enjoyable and successful. Virginia & Richard had wonderful and successful Antelope hunts under Your guidance they appreciated you and still talk of those hunts today.

Our 2014 Desert Big Horn Sheep Hunt (Romeo Hunt) was likely the stand out. Black Powder antelope and 2014 Elk hunts were also great adventures, to mention a few.

Darryl we want to thank You and Linda for all your help over the years, All The Best to You Both.
Thank you
Jim, Kathy, Richard & Virginia

ACKNOWLEDGMENTS

Without the following people, this book would never have been possible:

My wife Jodi, for her love and uncanny ability to understand me.
My children – Grace, Cash, and Sophia – for a taste of heaven on this side.
Kirt Darner for the spark and your friendship.
David Long for the chance.
Ryan Avery for believing in Rokslide.
Aron Snyder for your generosity.
Ben Walters and Kelly Andersson for getting this ball rolling.

And of course, my Lord Jesus for saving my soul
and giving me the abundant life He promised.

ABOUT THE AUTHOR

ROBBY DENNING GREW UP IN a mule deer hunting family just outside the small town of Iona, Idaho. He started hunting mule deer in the late 1970s, missing only one season in 35 years. At the age of 25, he gave up the pursuit of all other big game animals to focus on taking the best mule deer bucks possible. He began hunting the West on a do-it-yourself budget, scouting and hunting mule deer for about 60 days each year.

Robby loves the hunt as much as the kill – and the entire process from research to scouting to hunting to processing his own venison. He's killed four bucks over 200 inches in the last 15 seasons, mostly on easily obtained tags, and dozens of other bucks between 170" and 190". He owns and operates a public-land scouting service and a private-land outfitting business, and is co-owner of the huge online hunting site, Rokslide.com. Robby has scouted and hunted thousands of square miles of mule deer country across Idaho, Utah, Colorado, Wyoming, Montana, and Nevada. To him, the weapon of choice is just a means to an end; he will hunt with bow, rifle, or muzzleloader – whatever it takes to create an opportunity to take a great mule deer. He is also a published writer for several nationally recognized magazines and publishes weekly on his blog at Rokslide.com, which garnered two million hits in its first 12 months. Robby believes all of creation is from God for man to manage and respect, and through which to know its Creator.

PREFACE

Mule deer hunting to me is more than the hunt. it's become my life in so many ways – my pleasure, my pain, my passion, my nemesis – and still it grows. I've even asked God to take it away as He pleases, but every day it's still there, calling me to the next day I'll hunt again.

As I write this, I just closed the books on my 37th season of hunting mule deer. It was 24 years ago that I made the conscious decision to dedicate my life to the pursuit of big mule deer – a golden decision for me. Contained in the following pages is that journey. You will follow me into mule deer country. You will experience what I've experienced and you will learn what I have learned. You will close this book with the skills to kill the best buck of your life.

INTRODUCTION

THE ONE THAT STARTED IT ALL

I sat in the deep snow and pulled my knees to my chest. Resting my head on my forearms, I watched the tears drip from my cheeks. I closed my eyes and began to pray....

It was October 20, 1996. Although I'd been hunting mule deer with my father since the late '70s, this was day that mule deer hunting would truly change my life.

I'd been tracking a buck that I believed was a giant I'd first seen in early August. He was a big non-typical scoring over 230 inches gross on the Boone and Crockett scale. This was the 14th day I had hunted him. The last six days – packed in by horseback five miles and alone – I had hunted in the worst kind of weather: snow, sub-freezing temperatures, and at times, blizzard conditions.

I had cut the track not long after sunrise in some heavy aspen and conifer a few miles from my camp. My spirits lifted at the sight of the fresh blocky track characteristic of an older heavy-bodied buck. I checked the wind and terrain and made an educated guess on where he might be headed, and then set out after him.

1

He navigated the terrain without exposing himself in the occasional opening where a rifleman could get a shot, another indication he was an older buck. A half-mile later, he turned north to avoid the open and skirted the top of a small aspen-choked basin. The wind was wrong, so I climbed above the track and headed north hoping to catch him below me unaware of his tracker.

When I reached the northern rim of the basin and dropped down to check his track, I found he'd crossed the rim and headed down a 40-degree spruce-covered slope toward some finger ridges below. I figured he'd bed on those ridges for the day. I quickened my pace as I zigzagged across the track hoping to catch him before he bedded.

I reached the first bench above the finger ridges within 30 minutes. His track slowed, so I slowed too. I could see he was sneaking a few bites of the occasional browse sticking above the 10 inches of snow as he prepared to bed down. I checked my rifle – scope clear, safety free, and a shell in the chamber – and kept my eyes ahead, glancing at the track only occasionally. This hunt could be over any second if I played my cards right. I felt as alive as a man could feel.

Then I saw the other tracks. Coming from the east were the fresh boot tracks of another hunter. My heart crashed into my stomach. I'd seen quite a few hunters that week; elk season was open and most of those hunters would be carrying deer tags.

I continued on, watching for both hunter and buck. I'd walked only a short distance when I noticed the buck had broken into a run. It was clear that he'd heard or seen the other hunter, whose long stride indicated he was moving way too fast to catch a buck off guard. I followed a few hundred yards farther, but I could see the guy had thoroughly spooked the buck.

In that steep mountainous terrain, the buck would win. I'd learned too many times before that a frightened mule deer buck is nearly impossible to stay with in that type of country. He can put several miles – eight hours of walking for a man – between himself and his pursuer in an hour or less. In this kind of weather, I could not survive the night without shelter if darkness fell and I was too far from camp to return.

Crushed, I sat in the deep snow and began that prayer. I still had one day of season to hunt, but I had no strength left – as the tears on my face showed. I'd hunted mule deer for 30 days every year for the last six seasons, but had yet to kill a really big deer. I wanted to quit forever, right then and there.

I asked the good Lord for strength....

Drying my eyes, I stood and started the hike back up and south toward the rim of the aspen-choked basin. Maybe by some miracle, the buck would return to his home country before I had to pack out the next day.

Thirty minutes later, I stood on the rim overlooking the basin where I'd cut the track a few hours earlier. Within just seconds, I spotted a deer with my naked eye barely visible standing broadside in the aspen tangle 300 yards below me. I quickly put my old 8x42 Pentax binoculars to my eyes. Instantly I could see it was the giant! The buck I'd been tracking all morning had been the wrong buck.

I dropped onto my belly and crawled forward to clear the rise in front of me. Settling my scope on the hole in the brush where the buck stood, I could clearly see his incredible Boone and Crockett frame with more points than I could count in the few seconds I had to make the shot. I steadied the crosshairs and touched the trigger on my old Sako 7-mag.

The heavy snow muffled my shot. I quickly chambered a second round and settled back on the buck. He was absolutely motionless, still standing but now staring toward me. I took a short breath, touched the trigger, and then settled again. He was gone! I watched for a while as a nervous feeling crept over me; 300 yards in hunting conditions is no chip shot, and I feared that I'd just missed the biggest deer I'd ever seen.

I made my way down into the basin trying to keep a line of sight to where the buck had been standing. Approaching the tangle, I was exhilarated to see a blood-soaked skid trail headed down the mountain. Twenty yards below in some brush protruded the antler of the best buck – even to this day – that I've ever seen on the hoof. I dropped onto my rear and slid down the slope. As I knelt and touched the buck I'd pursued for two seasons, I praised God for not letting me quit.

That was nearly 20 years ago. As I write this now, I'm taken back to that very moment. My heart races a bit still, and there is a tingle on my skin. That was the buck that started it all for me. It changed the trajectory of my life. I knew that day, Lord willin', I'd spend my life pursuing big mule deer. Here and now, the fire still burns.

MY ROOTS

I was born in 1969. I grew up in the '70s, a time when mule deer hunting was changing. The boom was over, but deer hunting was still pretty good. Deer drives, group hunts, 4x4's, and 30.06 rifles were the tactics and equipment of the day. My dad and his three brothers all owned binoculars, but didn't use them much. We typically did a stand and a push in the morning, then hunted near and from the road the rest of the day.

They weren't lazy by any means – that is how it was done in the day. My dad was the buck hunter of the bunch. All of his brothers had taken nice deer, but it was Dad who had taken the most. Cool, calm, and collected, he was able to make the shots when it counted. Hunting in groups, the best shot usually got the big one.

It was my grandpa, Ed Denning, who really started buck fever in the Denning clan, but it really started for him in the islands of the Pacific.

He was in the Second Marine Division fighting against Japan in World War II. Grandpa was, among other duties, a sniper. That meant he had a scope when the other enlisted men had open sights. He became a fantastic shot. When your quarry can shoot back, you develop a quickness and precision that can't be learned any other way. Grandpa brought those shooting skills home with him. He was a genuinely great shot. It had become instinct for him to be a great shot. By the late '50s, his four sons were old enough to hunt. They all cut their teeth in some of the best Boone and

BESIDE THE PIER, two of the many Marines tumbled onto the reef by sinking boats work their way slowly toward the beach through intense Japanese fire, which seems to come from all directions.

Crockett country in the West. Get a map and draw a 50-mile circle around Soda Springs, Idaho, then check the record books and you'll see what I mean. In the day, some true giants were regularly coming out of this area. It was a mix of aspen, sage, rimrock, and buckbrush – prime buck habitat – and the country where I later learned to hunt mule deer.

They hunted it harder than most and over the years the racks piled up.

Grandpa made many a great shot during those days – 300 yards on running bucks, head shots, standing shots, shots with no time to think, long shots with no conscious range estimation – just let the mind take over and shoot – and my dad saw it all. It shaped him as a rifleman.

That was in the 1960s, a time when most people agree that big mule deer were at their peak. Grandpa, Dad, and his three brothers got to experience an era that will never come again. It seems my dad was the most interested in big mule deer. There were a few elk around then and as it is even now, elk drew a few of the Denning clan away from focusing on big mule deer. Dad hunted elk, but given the chance, he was all about chasing bucks.

My dad was one of those heroes of the era who wasn't afraid to bring a child into the world while he was still very young. He was 19 and my mom was 18 when I was born. This meant my earliest memories of him were when he was in his early twenties. I remember he'd fiddle with guns after work in the evening – aught sixes, .243s, muzzleloaders, 300 Winchester Magnums, .22 rifles and pistols – he liked them all and shot them all. My grandpa was a mechanic and built his own reloading equipment (go figure!) We'd spend many evenings in his basement working up loads.

I remember one load Dad was working on. He was shooting a 30.06 then and was on a quest for speed. He and Grandpa kept piling the powder into the military surplus cases until they could barely seat the bullets. At the range, Dad shot the gun and by the extra recoil he felt, was just sure he'd broken through 3,000 feet per second – something only the magnums of the era could do. When we got home and Dad started cleaning the gun, he found a big crack behind the action in the stock (what would you expect from a guy who uses homemade reloading equipment?) He had to back that load off a few grains. I later inherited that gun as my first deer rifle and every time I'd see that crack, I'd think about how "cool" my dad was.

He would often load my sister and me in the truck and take us shooting. I don't remember when I first shot a gun; it likely wasn't a memorable event as Dad was always working with guns. When fall would roll around, he and my uncle Mark – who lived right next to us – would gather up the horses, guns, and gear, and head for the buck country. I was too little to go, but I have memories of bucks hanging in the garage after those hunts and Dad retelling the stories.

It was just a few years later, when I was about 8 years old, that Dad started taking me on some of his mule deer hunts. He would wake me hours before sunrise and drive us to the sagebrush hills east of Idaho Falls, Idaho. It was cold and for the most part I was bored, but he was planting a seed as good fathers do. Nearly 40 years later, I realize just how unselfish that was. I didn't

realize at the time how much he was sacrificing to bring me along. I was always cold, and if I wasn't crying, I was still making way too much noise for him to ever get onto a buck. He kept me close to the road and the truck for safety, and I'm sure his success rate plummeted, but still he took me and I love him dearly for that.

I remember one fall about 1977 or '78 when Dad invited me and my little sister to deer camp. Grandpa, Dad, and his brothers had set up an epic camp in some southeast Idaho aspen country, complete with wall tent, woodburning stove, horses, and enough groceries to feed Patton's army. It was reachable by car, so my mom drove us up in her '64 Chevy Impala. Once there, I was like an ADD kid who'd forgotten to take his pills. I'd brought my new Benjamin pellet gun along and no living thing was safe (including humans.)

I explored the forest around camp, shot at pine hens (grouse), burned my hand on the stove, and accidentally loosed Grandpa's horse, Daisy. Mom kept us in camp while Dad hunted a few miles away on horseback with his brothers. Dad killed a beautiful 190" gross typical buck spreading 28" on that hunt. These were the kind of bucks that Boone and Crockett had in mind when they wrote the books; he was simply gorgeous. Dad hung the buck from a game pole in camp and even let me shoot it in the eye (the only place he said you could kill a buck with a pellet gun) for practice. Oh, the sweet memories I have of him and deer camp.

Over the next few years, he continued to take me on some of his hunts. He always talked about how smart big mature mule deer bucks were. He told stories of bucks hiding on the ground as his brothers walked close by. He had tales of bucks so big that he thought they were bull elk (my uncle Mark still ribs him about one of those giants Dad let get away), and of course stories of the ones that didn't get away. I listened closely and by the time I was 16 and hunting some on my own, I realized just how special big mule deer were. I also discovered how much I enjoyed hunting them. Dad always had a mantra about killing big mule deer:

"Anybody can get lucky and kill a big mule deer once in a lifetime, but very few people can do it twice. For that to happen, you have to do it on purpose." Those words sank in deep and later on became the challenge I wanted to meet.

Dad, always a good marksman, put this southeast Idaho buck on his nose with one shot as the buck trotted straight away at 100 yards.

Then there was my friend Cary Hansen, who was the local celebrity buck hunter of the day. He was nearly a decade older than me and one of the nicest guys I've ever known. Cary was kind enough to take me along on some of his buck hunts. I'd follow him around the southeast Idaho foothills like a good dog follows its owner.

Cary had a 7-mag but I had only an aught-six. He was an expert on a dirt bike but I just rode an old three-wheeler (Cary nicknamed me "The Irrigator"). He also showed me how far you could really go in a chained-up Ford pickup. That was before there were many off-road restrictions, and I'm ashamed to admit that we made more than a few new ones.

Cary Hansen was one of my early mentors and was a great buck hunter.

Cary was an excellent shot. When a buck would jump up, I was usually firing wildly from the ground to the sky. Cary would just settle down and kill him. He showed me by example how to make shots when the pressure was on.

Although I just fumbled along in his shadow, I learned so much about buck hunting from him. Cary taught me about hunting the rut and how to hunt the quakies – quaking aspen – where so many big bucks hide during the season.

During deer season, Cary's truck was always the envy of the town.

Cary with a buck he took at 600 yards in the days before rangefinders and range-compensating scopes. That's our friend Alan Barrus at Cary's side.

My old friend Cary Hansen was the local celebrity buck hunter back in the day. He took me on several of his hunts in the late '80s where he killed these bucks. I couldn't hit a semi-truck at 10 paces back then but he was kind enough to let me in the photos. Big bucks like these on OTC hunts were a little more common back then, though certainly not easy to kill. That's my friend Darin Bergeman with me there.

I cherish all those memories and am so thankful that he was willing to take a loud-mouthed teenager like me along. I likely wouldn't have chosen this path I'm on if it weren't for my friend Cary Hansen. I love him like a brother. I hope we get to hunt together at least one more time in this life. When we get to heaven, I'm going to find Cary and we'll head for the buck country, just like in the good ol' days.

That was in the mid-1980s and people were starting to hunt mule deer in the most remote places they could find – places that only a few years before rarely if ever saw a mule deer hunter. Around that time, Ike Ellis – who later became somewhat of a mentor to me – killed a fantastic southeast Idaho typical netting 211-2/8" Boone and Crockett. He killed that buck in the high country just a mile or so from where my family hunted the lower brush country.

Suddenly every serious hunter I knew, including me, wanted to hunt the high and lonesome. I wasn't as interested in hunting the lower elevation brush country I'd grown up on. I wanted to be on the highest farthest peak looking over several Boone and Crockett bucks a week.

Ike Ellis' fantastic 211-2/8" net Boone and Crocket Typical from southeast Idaho. This buck lit my fire.

I started investing my time in breaking horses, collecting gear, and scouting. I read everything I could on mule deer and studied the most successful hunters out there. I began finding some pretty big deer and although I hadn't killed one, I was slowly starting to get traction.

In 1991 I applied for my first out-of-state deer tag in Wyoming, something my father had done only once in his lifetime. He scratched his head and asked why would I quit hunting all the country I'd grown up in?

"I'm not quitting, I'll hunt both!" was my answer.

As a good dad always does, he got involved in my new high-country pursuits. He even backpacked with me five miles into Wyoming's Hoback Range to scout deer one summer, just a few months after he'd had serious back surgery.

The next two years, 1991 and 1992, I found several really good bucks – including a 200" non-typical – but again they escaped me. I was committed to succeed (and was really starting to enjoy the hunt beyond just antlers) so I kept on, undeterred. Then the winter of 1992-93 hit. It devastated mule deer herds across the West and is still the worst I've seen. Mule deer hunting got really tough after that but thankfully, I just couldn't accept the fact that the good times were really over.

14

I hunted for three more seasons, taking average bucks each year. Then in the summer of 1995, I started seeing a few really big bucks showing back up in the herd (not uncommon after killer winters, as only the best survive.) It was the season of 1996 – after six years of complete focus on hunting big mule deer – that I took my first really big buck, the one in the opening story of this book.

I was alone when I killed that buck but true to form, Dad made his way to camp – five miles on horseback in a snowstorm – to help me get the buck and the camp out. There was no one else in the world I would rather have had there for the moment. Back at camp that night, we cooked tenderloin and onions on the woodburner and talked about all our deer hunts. Sitting there with him in my old Army tent, I knew that he loved me and I loved him. Even if for just one night, I was the luckiest man alive.

It was only a few short years later that his earlier back surgery would cause complications that would prevent him from ever riding a horse or hunting backcountry bucks again. I remember our last backcountry hunt in 1998; he was in severe pain and we had to leave early. Riding back to the truck, I knew I was losing my hunting partner – and I did. I'll never be able to replace him, ever. I thank God for the times in mule deer country that we shared.

Up until that point, I was just trying to complete a goal of killing a really big deer, but that buck changed it from a goal to a lifelong pursuit. I'd learned that it was possible to get beyond luck and kill a big mule deer on purpose, just as Dad had said. I'm so thankful for those years he invested in me. Without him, I don't know what I'd be doing in life; and you'd likely be watching TV right now!

Decades later, the desire is still there and probably stronger than ever. I hope to kindle something similar in you. If more people care about big mule deer, then their chances of surviving and even thriving in an ever-changing world are more likely.

PART I: ICON OF THE WEST

WHY WE ARE DRAWN

While I love big bull elk, full-curl bighorn sheep, river-run salmon, Western whitetails, and record-smashing blacktail deer, nothing embodies the West like mule deer. Ask most hunters what is the hardest trophy to take in North America and most will say a big mule deer. While I'm not here to argue whether that is true or not – big bull elk are very tough to kill, full-curl rams are certainly no pushover, and big whitetail bucks annually elude millions of hunters – for one reason or another, big mule deer seem to have captured the hearts and minds of generations of hunters.

Could it be the fact that they grow the largest antlers of deer in North America? I realize elk and moose are "deer" but c'mon, everyone thinks of them as elk and moose, right?

Maybe it's because they've declined in recent decades while other species have flourished; everyone loves the underdog, and anything that is rare is valuable.

17

Could it be that many big mule deer inhabit some of the most gorgeous country God created on earth, the Rocky Mountains? Is it because they symbolize all that is the West? I think it is for all these reasons and more.

It's easy to believe that many people pursue big mule deer for their antlers. While that may be true, for me it has become something more. To me, to hunt mule deer successfully is to become part of their environment and their pace of life. They are a completely different creature than a human (if you want to call us a creature.) We can think, reason, and use tools but physically, we are nothing by comparison. A big mule deer can weigh 350 pounds on the hoof and is in peak physical condition most of his life. Imagine a 350-pound man in peak condition able to sprint 40 miles per hour, survive weeks of sub-zero temperatures, and with hearing, eyesight, and scent detection dozens to hundreds of times better than yours or mine. You get the picture.

To kill big mule deer, you have to immerse yourself in their world and you have to become like them: always watching, always listening, always perceiving, always learning. If you're lucky, you'll never take your best buck from a pickup truck or an ATV as that can only happen once in several lifetimes. If you're lucky, you'll take your best buck by learning to become part of their world. Then the action is repeatable.

I killed this big 250+ pound buck while moving slowly through deer country. He later lab-aged at four years old.

In mule deer country, we are strangers in a strange land; a land of silence, scent, vision, and perception that we cannot achieve. If it weren't for our tools and our brains, we'd never succeed. We can improve our skills, but we can't master the mule deer. To me, that is why we are drawn.

WHAT IS A "BIG" MULE DEER

As the term "Big" is in the title of this book, I need to explain what exactly that means. If you study older bucks as long as I have, you'll find that behavior-wise, they are a subset of the species. They behave completely differently from the rest of the herd, and it's why so few hunters are successful at killing them. Here is my definition of a "Big" mule deer.

□   **Age:** This is one of three critical factors that determine the size of a mule deer buck. I list it first because without age, it is very unusual for any buck to become big. Because I've lab-aged1 nearly all my big bucks (more than 20), and those of many other hunters, I have a pretty good barometer of how old big bucks are. I've found that virtually all big mule deer are at least four years old. There are cases of a few Boone and Crockett bucks in the books that were three years old, but they are extremely rare. For a buck to get big, he needs four candles on his birthday cake.

☐ **Body Size**. While size can vary according to latitude (Bergmann's Law says the farther north you move, the bigger the bodies of mammals become), all the bucks I've aged that are at least 4 years old have big bodies for the country they came from. They will be big enough that you will notice their size almost immediately, often before you've even noticed the antlers. They'll be longer, taller, and just plain bigger than other deer. I've even weighed several of my bucks on good scales. Dressed, they range between 200 and 285 pounds, which figures out to be around 250 to 350 pounds on the hoof. It takes at least four years for a buck to

---

1 Lab-aging is a specialized technique done by a qualified lab that dissects an extracted tooth allowing the technician to count the annual rings present in the tooth. It is the gold standard among wildlife professionals in accurately determining the age of deer. See my outfitting website at wescout4u.com for more information on having your buck lab-aged.

reach this size, and they typically get heavier up until their last year or so of life.

☐ **Antler Diameter** (or heaviness). While I love the record books, there are other "inches" that constitute a big mule deer. The pedicles from which the antlers grow typically gain diameter as the buck ages, so no matter the score, if you kill a buck with antler bases of 5-6 inches, you've very likely killed a buck 4 years or older. There is something commanding about a heavy-antlered buck that spread, height, and score just can't make up for.

21

I've weighed many bucks, both mine and those of clients, on good scales. Field dressed, they'll come in at 200-285 pounds. Estimated live weight will be 250 to 350 pounds.

This buck's right antler base was over 6 inches and his left over 5 inches. He later lab-aged at 8 years old. I estimated his live weight at over 300 pounds.

☐ **Antler width**. If you understand the record books, you'll see the most widely accepted scoring systems don't consider outside width in the final score. I understand that and don't challenge it. However, most of us do-it-yourself (DIY) hunters can't be so picky. Often when you see a big buck, the first thing that catches your eye is width. Not all big bucks are wide, but wide bucks are big! Wide bucks are also rare. I spend 60+ days a year looking exclusively for big mule deer and see only one or two that are 30" or wider each year. I have passed up a few wide bucks over the years, but only because they were young bucks with small bodies and light antlers.

☐ **Score**. I saved this one for last as I think it is less relevant these days than in the past. Big mule deer, especially those that make Boone and Crockett's All-Time list (minimum net score of 190" typical and 230" non-typical) are very very rare. How rare? I've spent 37 years in some of the best Boone and Crockett mule deer country in Idaho, Colorado,

Wyoming, Utah, and Nevada, yet I've seen only four or five typicals that would make the all-time list and zero – yes zero – non-typicals. It's because of this rarity that I don't list score first. If I did, you may not appreciate the fact that there are many "big" mule deer alive and well that won't make the book, yet 99 percent of us DIY-ers will be happy with them. However, I still use score in my definition of big. I think any buck that is 180" gross Boone and Crockett is big. Most hunters who see a buck like that on the hoof hands-down agree with me and will pass them up only if they've seen a bigger one in the area or have a very special draw tag. In all my scouting and hunting, I might see three to five bucks a year that exceed that size, so I know they're rare, and big.

A 191" gross Boone & Crockett mule deer

Spend a few decades and a thousand days in mule deer country then let me know if you agree or disagree with my definition. Unless you're very wealthy and can hunt the best of the West regularly, I'd bet you will agree.

For the rest of this book, if you read the word "big," I'm referring to a buck that is older, experienced in the way of the hunter, and has several of the characteristics given above. You may find the occasional exception – the 30" buck lab-aged at three years or the 10-year-old buck with 22" light antlers –

but by and large, if a mule deer is "big," he is rare and valuable and must be hunted differently than younger smaller bucks.

HOW MULE DEER HUNTING HAS CHANGED

Most mule deer hunters and experts agree that the 1950s and '60s were the peak of mule deer herds and big bucks. While theories abound on the reasons, most conclude that we may never see that era again.

Actually that is okay with me. I was born when I was born and that just so happened to be in the final years of that era. In a way, I'm *glad* I didn't experience it, because it would have spoiled me rotten. Not so much anymore, but in the '80s and '90s, I met many buck hunters who'd simply given up because "all the big bucks are gone." I remember hunters standing up at Fish and Game meetings angry because they would hunt three days and never see a thirty-incher like they had so commonly seen in the past. There were hunters around here who'd kill big bucks after work, just a few miles from town. Most of these guys just quit once the hunting got tough. I may have done the same if I had experienced the true heyday of mule deer like they had.

In the 1970s, mule deer herds were fairly stable, but big bucks were getting harder to kill. Formerly, many seasons were designed for the big buck hunter to be successful; seasons ran into late November and even December on over-the-counter (OTC) tags. Biologists were starting to trim those seasons back, as too many big bucks were being killed as technology and more free-time became common – even early scopes changed hunting more than you might think. There were some pretty hard winters around the West in the later half of the 1970s but herds bounced back fairly quickly. More people were also starting to travel farther to hunt mule deer.

The 1980s weren't a bad time for big deer. There were few ATVs and most seasons were fairly liberal with good tags easy to obtain. Any serious hunter could kill good bucks and didn't usually have to get far from a road to do it. There were few hunters serious enough to pack in 10 miles for just a mule deer.

Then in 1983, Kirt Darner released his book, *How to Find Giant Mule Deer*. While Kirt has had his troubles with the law (more on that later), no one can argue the fact that he inspired a generation of trophy mule deer hunters.

At the time, Kirt had killed over a dozen Boone and Crocket mule deer, a feat no one before or since has accomplished (only one of those deer has been disputed). Many hunters took great interest in that book, which became a bestseller in the "how-to" genre. Kirt sold over 20,000 copies, quite a feat for a self-published book in the days before the internet.

The famous back cover of Kirt Darner's book *How to Find Giant Bucks*

Before *Giant Bucks*, people thought Boone and Crockett bucks were nearly mythical and virtually no one believed that you could kill one on purpose. Well, Kirt had killed a dozen on purpose and detailed all his methods in the book. For the first time on a national scale, the trophy mule deer hunter was born.

Besides placing a greater focus on Boone and Crockett-producing counties and units, the book spawned the high-country hunter. Ridges and peaks that had been visited only by the occasional Basque sheepherder were now the destination of thousands of mule deer hunters. While the hunters wore cotton underwear, rarely used binoculars, and stood on the skyline, there were still enough undisturbed bucks that the new trophy hunters still killed some whoppers.

Just a few years later, a small new publication further changed the high country of Wyoming, Idaho, and Colorado: *Eastman's Hunting Journal* started by Mike Eastman. Stories and photos from regular guys with huge bucks taken in high lonely basins graced the pages. The serious hunters I knew hated Eastman's concept, but most relented and figured "If you can't beat 'em, join 'em."

Suddenly the high-country hunter was in vogue and hunters streamed into the Western wilderness country. Places such as Wyoming's Grey's River and Hoback, Colorado's federal Wilderness Areas, Idaho's Sawtooth Range, Utah's Wasatch, and Nevada's Ruby Mountains were the places to find big mule deer. I knew a few deer hunters who got in on the bounty. They were seeing and killing giant bucks like those that hadn't been seen since the 1960s.

Within a few years, the newly invented ATV was making its way to every ridgetop in the West and the high country was effectively shrinking. The decline in quality hunting – which had been characterized by easy-to-obtain tags, little competition, and quite a few big bucks – had begun.

By the time the killer winter of 1992-93 (the worst one I've seen in my life) hit, after five years of drought, the change was upon us. In '93 the best deer hunters I knew wore only frowns. Idaho, Colorado, Utah, Montana, Nevada, and Wyoming all had been affected. Many hunters quit, just plain quit.

There was a genuine sense of panic across the West and many people thought the mule deer would never recover. Organizations such as the Rocky Mountain Mule Deer Federation (the precursor to The Mule Deer Foundation) and others, along with thousands of hunters and state game agencies, rallied for the cause. More conservative management strategies were becoming common across the West. Colorado, the nation's mule deer factory, implemented a three-day season, Idaho dumped its OTC rut hunts, Utah replaced rifle rut hunts with muzzleloader hunts and completely closed some units, and every state switched more OTC hunts to limited quota hunts. All these efforts, along with an improvement in weather, helped get big mule deer bucks back on their feet, but the big picture had really changed for the individual trophy hunter. It was getting tougher to kill big mule deer, as tags were fewer, the odds of drawing for limited quota hunts – while always tough – were worsening, and more hunters were forced into the remaining OTC units.

Anything rare is valuable (have you heard of the rare Kopi Luwak coffee made by the digestion of coffee beans through the Asian Palm Civet cat in Indonesia – people pay $75 a cup!)

With big mule deer harder to come by, outfitters and landowners (and some state game agencies) began to focus on growing trophy bucks. It was widely agreed that in the mid-1990s that the only North American big game trophy that couldn't be bought was a mule deer. Giant elk, sheep, whitetails, antelope, and bears were accessible to the hunter with a big wallet, but mule deer for the most part were not.

With the focus on trophy management and the realization by state game agencies that private landowners held some of the most valuable habitat (especially winter range) for mule deer, landowner tag systems were born or expanded. Outfitters leased the best private land and implemented management strategies to grow more big bucks. This meant they had to sell fewer hunts, so prices doubled, tripled, and quadrupled. Suddenly, some people could actually buy a trophy mule deer.

The '90s also saw an expansion of elk herds across the West as a result of conservation, land-use practices, and habitat change that favored elk more than mule deer. While opinions on the competition of elk versus mule deer abound, most people agree that more elk means fewer mule deer – and in many places that is holding true.

With the increased interest in big gnarly bucks, media – including magazines and the newly born web – further increased interest. Regular everyday hunters could get national attention on the cover of a magazine where before, only a few hunting superstars could do that.

With the war on terror starting in 2001 and the invasion of Afghanistan, our military fought its first mountain war since Korea fifty years earlier. The military dumped billions into improving outdated gear, and in just a few short years, mountain gear for hunters improved by leaps and bounds. Hunters could stay longer and hunt harder than ever before.

With the rise of the internet, information on trophy mule deer hunts became widely available. A small publication begun in 1995 by Garth Carter, "The Huntin' Fool," became a leader in providing trophy hunting info to the common man. Other media jumped on board, and draw odds for the new limited-quota units went from low to dismal to horrible.

During this time, more hunters began to look to primitive weapon hunts to hunt mule deer. Good rifle hunts were very hard to draw, but archery and muzzleloader hunters could hunt those same units without waiting years for a tag. For probably the first time since the Ute Indian era, some giant mule deer began to fall to bowhunters (and muzzleloaders) in significant numbers. It's no coincidence to me that the number one big mule deer hunter currently is an archer from Arizona, Randy Ulmer. He's shown the world that a modern compound bow can put more big mule deer on the ground than a modern firearm for an individual hunter.

As I write this, I'd say the current state of mule deer is pretty good. In a few places, it's much better (if you can get a tag), some places it's bad, but in most places it's fairly stable. On average, it's not as good as it was in the '80s but is better than in the '90s. There is enough public interest for the species to get the attention and help that mule deer need. There is certainly the problem of shrinking habitat, and over the long term that could be detrimental to not just mule deer but the elk, too. However, I think mule deer are more adaptable than previously thought. Few places have seen the expansion of human development into mule deer habitat like Colorado, but their mule deer, in part because of more conservative management, are doing well. Most states are managing mule deer better with laws and initiatives to protect mule deer and improve habitat. It seems that if the habitat is functioning, a little management goes a long way in helping mule deer, especially mature buck numbers. In some units, just a small decrease in hunting pressure makes a big difference.

Weather is always the wild card, and it's hard to predict how it will affect the mule deer's future. In the Rocky Mountains, hard winters affect mule deer greatly, as does long-term drought, but they both always have. Wolves are another wild card. They've affected elk herds more than mule deer but only time will tell. We're managing wolves through hunting now, and I believe that if state game agencies are allowed to do their jobs – and there is not a fundamental shift in wolf management policies – a balance can be found.

Buck hunting always has ebbed and flowed and will continue to do so. While the easy bucks are mostly gone, don't lose heart. It's been just a few months since I've hunted an 8x9, 210" non-typical Idaho buck with greater than a 30" spread on an OTC hunt. I killed a 180" buck with a muzzleloader in Colorado just a week later, then ended the rifle season killing an 8-year-old (lab-aged) heavy Idaho buck with 6" bases on a hunt where I saw no other hunters in nine days. The big ones are still out there, and in enough numbers that a dedicated and adaptable hunter can kill more than a few of them.

If you want to take the best buck of your life, then you need to understand where we've come from and where we're going. You have to learn enough about mule deer that you can adapt to changes affecting them. In my hunting career, many changes – as detailed here – have affected mule deer, but I'm adapting, too. I can absolutely say I'm glad that I didn't give up even when things didn't look so great. I learned so much in those decades, enjoyed so many hunts, and even killed quite a few big deer. You can, too.

While mule deer will continue to ebb and flow, I certainly don't have a sky-is-falling attitude. If I believed what some hunters say, I'd feel guilty even hunting mule deer at all. I also believe the mule deer's future can be good if enough sportsmen care – and act on it. I think trophy hunters can bring a lot of help to the mule deer simply because we're the most passionate about them. Big mule deer bucks show up in numbers only when the whole herd is functioning. For that to happen, we have to care deeply. In part, that is why I'm writing this book – to bring a greater attention to the true Icon of the West, the mule deer.

PART II: MENTAL & PHYSICAL ASPECTS OF HUNTING BIG BUCKS

HUNTING FOR BIG MULE DEER IS VERY SIMILAR to any competitive sport. The big difference is that you're usually competing with yourself. Like any athletic pursuit, there is the mental game and the physical game to hunting for big mule deer, and you must master both. First, let's tackle the mental side of our mule deer game.

THE MENTAL: WHY YOU HAVE TO CHANGE TO BE SUCCESSFUL

Because the easy bucks are gone, you can't employ the strategies of yesteryear if you want to put a big mule deer in your freezer and on your wall. You can't hunt like everyone else or you'll get the same results they do, which is pretty dismal. Most states post success rates on bucks around 10-20 percent. If you did the math on big mule deer, I'd guess it's around 1 percent, meaning 1 percent of hunters are intentionally (key word, think about it) killing big mule deer. To join that 1 percent, you have to change your thinking.

When I get the opportunity to talk with other mule deer hunters, I find that I'm doing things differently, often way differently, than the vast majority of hunters out there. I may be hunting many of the same places, but I'm hunting them differently. That is why my results are 99 percent different from average, and it's not just me. I know several dedicated hunters who kill a big mule deer nearly every year. You can join those ranks if you're willing to open your mind and learn. For some hunters, it's very hard to give up what they've been taught for their entire lives. However, unless they're killing big mule deer yearly, they're going to have to change tactics. I grew up with a great hunter as my teacher – my dad – but because mule deer hunting is different now, I had to let go of some things I'd learned. You might, too.

Big mule deer are a sub-set of the species and behave differently than the rest of the herd. Consequently, they must be hunted differently. Three-year-old and younger bucks are the ones that give mule deer a bad reputation. They rarely go nocturnal during hunting season, wander more, like the open country, and stop to look back after being spooked. Consequently, many hunters think mule deer bucks are dumb. Other hunters falsely assume there are only young bucks in the herd, because that is all they ever see (some of these hunters are the ones always calling for limited draw hunts, closing the deer season, and generally making it harder on the rest of us.)

I started reading and studying trophy mule deer hunters in my late teens – hunters including Walt Prothero of Utah, Ted Riggs of Arizona, Albert Ellis of Wyoming, and at the top of the heap, my friend Kirt Darner. If you know Kirt, author of *How to Find Giant Bucks*, you'll know he's had his troubles with the law, so I'd better diverge a bit....

I'm very aware of those troubles; I testified at Kirt's sentencing hearing in January 2009 in Grants, New Mexico. You busybodies don't need to send me email with your theories on what Kirt's done or not done. I know the truth and I know the rumors. That's old news and Kirt has paid his debt to society. Just as this book went to print, Kirt received a Conditional Discharge from the State of New Mexico. The judge over the case dismissed all original charges after Kirt put in over 2700 hours of community service and paid heavy fines. Kirt is free to to hunt again and return to normal family life and hobbies. I think my friend has learned his lesson.

Some have told me it would be suicide to even mention my association with him in my first book. They could be right. However, I'd be lying if I ducked and ran, refusing to admit that much of what I learned about big deer in my early years came from Kirt's book and later, his friendship. I don't agree or condone or accept some of the things Kirt has done, but I also won't abandon him. He's my friend and if I ever make a mistake, I hope my friends stick by me.

Now back to other hunters I've studied: Dwight Schuh and his classic *Hunting Open Country Mule Deer*, Francis E. Sell's *The Deer Hunter's Guide*, Mike

Eastman, Randy Ulmer (the best of the day in my opinion), Chuck Adams, David Long, Myles Keller, Larry Benoit and his sons, Lanny, Lane, and Shane, and certainly many more I've forgotten. I learned many things from these men, but the most striking thing I learned is that they hunt differently than the masses and consequently have better success on big deer than the masses.

You may have noticed some of those names mentioned are those of Whitetail/Blacktail/Sitka deer hunters, and you'd be right. While mule deer are their own species inhabiting their own habitat, they are still deer and many of their behaviors are common with the rest of the deer family.

For example, reading about Larry Benoit and his sons' techniques for tracking big whitetails in the Northern Tier states, I realized that big mule deer can be tracked in the West using similar techniques, especially during the rut. Francis E. Sell's 1964 book, *The Deer Hunter's Guide*, focused on blacktails, but I've noticed big mule deer often have the same affinity for heavy cover in the West and the hunting techniques overlap.

Chuck Adams' stories on killing world-record Sitka deer showed me that even our northern-most deer can be hunted in open country if hunting pressure is virtually non-existent, just like some of the premium hunts in the West where tag numbers are extremely low.

If you're reading this book to up your game on big mule deer, open your mind to the fact that you may have to change your thinking about how they are hunted. Even if you were lucky enough to have been born and raised in the West, you have to accept the fact that you may not really know how to hunt big mule deer. I've hunted them for 37 years and feel like I'm just scratching the surface. If you're new to mule deer hunting, you actually may have the new-dog new-trick advantage over those who've hunted mule deer for a lifetime and are stuck in their ways.

FAULTY THINKING

Let me give you some examples of faulty thinking I find among hunters, thinking that I had to overcome to start killing big mule deer:

"If I hunt the wilderness, backcountry, and high country, I'll kill a big mule deer." While I prefer the high and lonesome, you have to accept the fact that old bucks in those areas are often the hardest to kill. They are completely undone at the sight, sound, or smell of a human compared with their compadres living closer to civilization. They'll vacate the immediate country if you spook them and may never come back that season. Older bucks also choose that type of country; it affords them many advantages over their predators (you're their top predator), including miles of visibility, steep slopes that are difficult to traverse quietly, air unpolluted by noise where sound carries great distances, finicky thermals, and other factors that make it tough to get close to big mule deer.

I find hunters making the mistake of packing in ten miles, then setting camp up on an open ridge that can be seen for miles around. They talk loudly, stand on the skyline, and let their scent blow into likely country. If they are on horses, they'll separate them, causing the horses to whinny, which can be heard miles away. I've made all those mistakes (and still do sometimes). Backcountry bucks won't put up with that. Just because they live far from civilization doesn't make them easier to hunt. I'd argue it makes it harder. You have to hunt backcountry bucks with all the stealth you can muster.

"If I could just get on private property, I could kill a big buck." Most private property is covered with roads, easy to access, and gets plenty of pressure from the landowner's friends and family. The landowner usually knows where the best bucks have been killed, so there are few safe zones. I've been an outfitter for 13 years operating solely on private property. I manage hunter numbers tightly and consequently grow a few big deer every year. Yet if I let an unguided hunter hunt the ranch, they usually never see the big bucks I've watched all summer, even when I send them to the exact spots where those bucks live. This happens frequently. Sometimes our season wraps up early, leaving me a few days to hunt. I've killed a few big deer, but for the most part I find the big bucks are hiding in heavy cover and difficult to kill. I must hunt carefully and diligently to kill those older bucks. Hunting well-managed private property is a real treat and can certainly improve your chances at tagging a great buck, but you have to hunt smart and hard, just like in the backcountry.

"Big mule deer live far from roads." This is related to the first point but is also faulty thinking. Big mule deer are almost always older than most of the herd. They've had years to learn their area, know where the threats come from and the best places to hide from predators. They are masters at finding areas where they can survive (part of why I'm personally drawn to them). While on average, age class increases the farther you get from a road (as long as you're still in mule deer country), there are many places close to roads where big mule deer live and thrive. I've killed two of my best Colorado bucks within a half-mile of paved public roads – one on moderately hunted public land and another on moderately hunted private land (heavy hunting pressure anywhere is just too much for even the big bucks to survive in number.)

In both cases, the bucks had found areas with enough cover, the right thermals, and the visual ability to detect 99 percent of hunters who might breach their safe zone. I've also scouted countless big bucks living close to

35

civilization in Idaho and Nevada, so I know it's a common behavior among big mule deer. In this day and age where hunting far from roads is in vogue, some bucks spend their hunting seasons living surprisingly close to roads. To kill big mule deer you have to hunt a lot where they exist. If you're not willing to hunt all the mule deer country where big bucks live, you're stacking the odds against yourself.

"If I could just draw a good tag I could kill a big buck." Whoa, hold it right there partner! That is a very big mistake. Hear me out on this one. There are more draw-hunts than ever now – and more people applying for those hunts. Many really big deer come from the draw units and end up on the pages of magazines and in every mule deer forum on the internet. Hunters who kill these deer aren't very protective of the information, because they know they will probably not get a tag again. Soon, everyone knows that unit X is the place to be. This causes us to think that all the big bucks come from those units and we're less motivated to hunt areas that have fewer big deer and more hunting pressure. Even worse, if you were lucky enough to draw a great tag and kill a great buck, you'll be so disappointed in a lesser unit that you'll likely give up and go elk hunting or golfing rather than grind it out and kill a big deer where anyone can hunt (which is more satisfying than killing them on a great unit). If you want to kill a big mule deer, you have to learn how to hunt them, and the only way to do that is to hunt every single year so you can learn everything possible. You will be successful on big mule deer if you learn everything you can. Only then will you be able to take full advantage of a great unit when you do draw (most of us will draw a few in our lifetimes), as you'll be fully prepared to hunt big mule deer. I've killed most of my big bucks in units where virtually anyone can hunt.

"There are big bucks in this unit, so there should be one where I'm hunting." I learned early on, and have had several top deer hunters agree, that just because you're in the buck country does not mean there is a big buck there. You can hunt smart and hard, but if there isn't a big deer where you're hunting, you won't kill one. You have to know enough mule deer country that you can spend your valuable time hunting where big bucks actually live. This means scouting and hunting enough that you've located individual bucks where you can focus your limited time and energy in those places. Studying Google Earth will surely show you buck honey holes, but until Google starts a live satellite feed (God forbid!) you will never know if a big mule deer lives there any given year until you scout and hunt the area.

That takes time but is how you can separate yourself from the masses. Most hunters try a place once, and then move on if they don't see a freak-antlered muley. Once I find good buck country, I check on it often, and sooner or later I find a big mule deer living there. Then I can confidently focus my time and energy on killing him. Some of these places won't hold a big buck for a decade then BAM! one shows up. That means nine out of ten years the place was a bust. I have to keep scouting and hunting hard to find the best bucks. If you don't live close to mule deer country, you can still be successful. You just have to accept the fact that it's likely going to take longer – but be encouraged. The fun is in the search, and I've met many mule deer hunters who don't live in the West but who do very well on big mule deer. I find these hunters all have one thing in common: they know their area. So should you.

Ponder these thoughts and make sure you're not chronically making these mistakes. Big mule deer are a completely different animal than what you might think. Unless you have already killed three or more big mule deer, you probably have to change your thinking.

WHY YOU HAVE TO FOCUS

A big mule deer hunter has to be one of the most focused big game hunters on the continent to be successful. I've already discussed how rare big bucks are. In my opinion, they are rarer than the rest of all of our big game species. If I want to kill a 350" bull elk, I could be hunting several areas with bulls like that as soon as next year on OTC or easy-to-draw tags. While I may not kill one, I know I'd see at least one. However, a 200" mule deer (to me, about the equivalent on the size scale as a 350" bull elk) would be much harder. I spend 60 days a year looking for big bucks and see only about one 200" or better buck every two or three years in units where I can get a tag. I don't waste much time scouting the premium units where so many of the big bucks we see in media are filmed, as I know I'll likely never get to hunt them.

Because big mule deer are so rare, if you want to kill one, you have to focus almost exclusively on them. Twenty years ago, I'd hunt bucks, bulls, and birds, and I'd fish for steelhead (which I love to do). At the end of each season, it seemed that I was doing fine on everything but big mule deer. I was always a day late and a dollar short. I enjoyed archery elk hunting and killed bulls almost every year, even in my early twenties. I love steelhead fishing, and while I'm no expert, if the fish were in the river I did fairly well. Few hunts have the action of wingshooting pheasants, quail, and gray partridge, and I spent many days in their pursuit. Spring turkey hunting is the next best thing to calling in bull elk, and I chased turkeys from northern to southern Idaho back in the day. Yet every year would close without my killing a big mule deer.

Once I married my precious wife Jodi in 2001, I had to get focused if I wanted to kill a big buck. Jodi is about the least demanding and lowest maintenance woman I've ever met, but I loved her and knew she was going to need more of my time if we wanted a great marriage. That time was going to have to come from somewhere.

I tried to do it all the first few years. She was a doll and supported me as much as she could, even trailing along on adventures with me. I remember her falling down in a Salmon River riffle while we fished for steelhead together. When I heard the splash, I looked over and could see only her belly sticking out of the water – she was five months pregnant! She also packed in with me on my summer mule deer scouting trips. Jodi is a backpacker but not a hunter. We truly enjoyed those trips together, and are starting to do more now that our three kids are getting older. However, it was becoming clear that if I wanted to kill a big buck, something had to give.

I first gave up elk hunting; that gave me back a week plus. As much as I love fishing for big trout and steelhead, I also relinquished that pursuit, save the trips we schedule together with the kids. That gave me back many weekends and of course gave me precious family times that beat any 7-pound trout or 17-pound steelhead. I quit hunting birds, too. The first year was tough, but come fall I was able to hunt 30 days for mule deer (not all at once of course) without wearing too much on Jodi. I also noticed my energy level was better. It's easy to dream all winter about hunting giant bucks for ten days straight but in reality, you have only so much mental energy to put to the task (notice I didn't say physical energy). All those other pursuits had been competing for that energy, and once I started focusing it on mule deer, I just did better.

Finally, big deer hunting is expensive. The horses, the gear, the tags, the trucks, and the travel all drain the bank account. Once I had a family, I couldn't be dipping into our livelihood just to hunt big deer. In my twenties, I could live in a small apartment with only enough clothes to fit in a box. While Jodi is pretty good with me, asking her to eat beans and rice six nights a week so I can afford to apply for Western tags was probably out of the question.

By focusing exclusively on mule deer, I was able to carve out enough days, energy, and finances to maximize my success. Many of the successful trophy mule deer hunters I know also follow the same thinking. Brian Latturner owns

39

the website MonsterMuleys.com (you should check it out if you haven't, it's one of the best online resources for mule deer), and is one of the most successful DIY big mule deer hunters that I know. He, too, focuses exclusively on hunting mule deer and has the skills and bucks to show for it.

If you really want to kill a big mule deer, you're going to have to focus virtually all your free time and energy on the pursuit. If you don't, you may never succeed. You might dabble in the pursuit and eventually take a big mule deer, but it could take 20 years or more. That's not a wise move, as few if any can stay motivated for 20 years. Those guys get discouraged after a couple seasons, give up, and go elk hunting. Don't be those guys. Focus!

Brian Latturner, founder of MonsterMuleys.com with a great muley buck. Brian hunts only mule deer and has the bucks to show it. His site's a great resource for every mule deer hunter.

HUNTING SOLO

As you read this book, you'll probably notice that I've killed most of my big deer while hunting alone. That would be true, but I didn't really plan it that way. Hunting for big mule deer tends be a loner's pursuit by nature. The reasons are varied.

It's hard to find someone equally as committed.

Before I say what I'm going to say, I want to be clear that if I had to choose between the welfare of my family and my walk with God or deer hunting, God and family would win every time. There's not a stinky old mule deer on the planet worth harming my most important relationships. However, I am very dedicated to the pursuit.

I find that most hunters are interested in killing a big mule deer. However, when they find out just how much sacrifice it really takes, the crowds thin dramatically.

The love of my life Jodi. She's says I might think about
buck hunting too much. I don't know about that, but
the country behind her is just too rocky for big bucks.

My life is my family's but because I'm married to a wonderful wife who
believes the same, when it's time to go deer hunting or scouting, she's behind
me. Occasionally I've missed my son's football game, or my two daughters'
recitals, or I've had to tell my boss that I can't make the meeting he planned,
endangering promotion and even my job. I've chosen to take unpaid vacation
time that could have been spent with my family, but then worked extra jobs in
the off season to make it up (I have three as I write this). I've already written
that I gave up other hunting and fishing pursuits so I could fully commit to the
pursuit of killing big mule deer. On occasion, I've come home from a nine-day
hunt, repacked my gear, and then headed back out again while watching my
supportive family wave goodbye again in the rear-view mirror. I've hunted
until I'm so tired and grouchy that it takes a week to snap out of it. I've hunted
way beyond the point of enjoyment many times, because that simply is what it
took to be successful.

When you're this committed, it's very difficult to go along with someone who's just there for the experience. In fact, they usually just uninvite themselves in one way or another, and you're left alone on the mountain. This has happened to me many times over the decades and is the primary reason I end up hunting alone.

Attitude

Even if someone is equally as committed, if they don't have a good attitude throughout the hunt, you'll be hamstrung. Like everything in life, your attitude pretty much ensures your success or failure. I've hunted with others who become down-in-the-mouth about buck hunting, and it wears on me. They might complain about Fish and Game's management strategies, how they wished they could have hunted 30 years ago when the hunting was better, how the guys on the other ridge are screwing up the hunt, blah, blah, blah. While I've been guilty of slipping into bad attitudes, I've learned that I must snap out of it or my hunt is doomed. Sometimes I have to take a day off during the hunt to recover mentally and physically. Oddly I find that someone with a bad attitude thinks that's a wasted day, further increasing the friction in camp. Also, if I continue to hold out for a big deer yet the other guy thinks he has to kill something to be successful, we end up in further disagreement. To plan a hunt with someone who has a bad attitude is just hunt suicide. You'll end up either trying to ignore the person or trying to cheer them up, both of which will wear you down.

Selfishness

Because big buck hunting is so tough and big bucks so rare, if you're not equally yoked with your hunting partner, you'll likely feel a twinge of selfishness or downright jealousy if he puts the smack on a big buck and you don't. This is the ugly side of human nature, but I'd be a liar if I didn't mention it. Sometimes I hunt alone because I know I'm just not man enough to let someone who hasn't done the work have a chance at something I've worked so hard for. I'm not saying it's right, I'm just saying it's true.

Living alone for a week in the backcountry isn't for everyone

Two are better than one

Now after saying all this, I want to confirm that if you find a good hunting partner, you're better off hunting with another person. King Solomon in all his God-given wisdom said this in the Bible:

"Two are better than one,

Because they have a good reward for their labor.

For if they fall, one will lift up his companion.

But woe to him who is alone when he falls,

For he has no one to help him up."

Ecclesiastes 4: 9-10

That's as true today as when he wrote it 900 years before Christ.

First, in the literal sense, you could get hurt while hunting alone. Hunting with a good hunting partner increases your safety in mule deer country and especially the backcountry. I'm no fool in thinking nothing can happen to me when hunting alone – it could. When I'm hunting with a friend, I'm just plain safer.

More likely, though, you're going to fall down mentally. Big buck hunting is tough and can also be very boring. Sometimes you'll question your own sanity in the pursuit. Having an equally yoked partner along will greatly increase your mental strength. I've hunted 13 days straight with a partner and was ready for more. Yet another time I hunted 14 days straight alone and was a basket case by the time I got back to the truck. You can't hunt effectively unless you're mentally in the game, and a good hunting partner really helps.

Also, if you're both in the game together, you can arrive at a place where you're just as happy if your partner gets the big one. You won't feel cheated in the slightest way, as you'll both understand that the big buck likely would never have been taken had you not worked together.

My friend Kevin took this fantastic typical on a backcountry hunt we made a few years back. We found the buck the previous day, but he got away. The next day, we finally bedded him in the heavy cover. I cut off his lower escape route while Kevin waited above for the buck to stand. Nearly eight hours later he did, and Kevin put the hammer down. I can honestly say that I was as excited for him to kill the buck as if I had killed it myself. The buck was 33" wide, grossed 190" Boone and Crockett, and lab-aged at five years old.

Besides my father, Doug, I've hunted with four men who really added to the experience. I love and care about each of these people and look forward to the day when we can hunt again. I hunted with Kevin Kenny of Idaho Falls for years. He's an intelligent hunter with the patience of a mule – and he's a great shot. We took many a good buck together and I cherish those memories.

I've hunted with Trevor Carlson of Great Falls, Montana on several Montana hunts. His youth, mental toughness, and enthusiasm to learn about big deer were a great encouragement to me.

Ryan Pimentel and I have been friends for years. He's one of the best bowhunters I know. In 2010 we hunted together for a few weeks in the Wyoming backcountry for a 200" buck we named A.D.D. for attention deficit disorder. Because of Ryan's always-good attitude, physical toughness (this guy hunted with a fever well over 100 degrees on one of the nastiest mountains I've ever been on), and just plain willingness to learn, that hunt was one of the best hunts of my life. Although A.D.D. moved at all hours of the day (hence the name), and we had him in both rifle and archery range several times, we still never killed him. However, the memories will last a lifetime.

Ryan Pimentel and I chasing a 200" Wyoming buck back in 2010
in some incredibly steep country. Ryan teases me about my vest.
I'd forgotten mine and found this one on the highway where
a road crew had been working. Oh well, at least I was legal.

Kirt Darner of Crawford, Colorado, has been a mentor to me since I was in my twenties. I know he's had his troubles but Kirt's been nothing but good to me and my family. In 2000, I guided some hunters for Kirt's American Outfitters operation. We killed this Colorado buck on that hunt.

In 2004 Kirt and I made another Colorado hunt together. It was one of the most memorable hunts of my life. It was during the heated election between George W. Bush and John Kerry; Kirt is quite the card and posted this sign outside our wall tent. As people drove by, I noticed that they either smiled and waved with their whole hand or just frowned and waved with part of their hand.

The third morning of the hunt, Kirt set an ambush in a nasty draw choked with oakbrush and junipers while I hunted a basin a mile to the south. When I heard a shot at 8:30 a.m. from the draw, I figured I better find my knife. Then I heard seven more shots and knew something was wrong.

When I met Kirt on the road, he frowned and said he had wounded a good buck. That's not like Kirt, so I carved a bullseye in an aspen at 100 yards and we checked the rifle. His first bullet hit 4 inches low and 5 inches right, so we re-sighted the gun. Kirt then put two more in the tree less than an inch apart.

"He better stay out of the way now," he chuckled as we hiked back toward the draw.

Kirt's plan was to follow the track while I kept a lookout from a few steps behind him. He'd have to concentrate on the ground and might not see the buck in time to get a shot. It hadn't rained or snowed in a week and I was at least skeptical.

An hour later, Kirt finally pointed to a smear in the dirt and said that was the buck's track. There was no blood, and deer tracks were everywhere. I figured he must know what he was doing, so I followed a few yards behind, eyes peeled and rifle ready. He kept telling me the buck was walking funny and thought he'd wounded a leg. I couldn't even tell if they were the same tracks, let alone how the buck was walking.

Over the next hour, the buck zigzagged from cover to cover, leading us a mile over a mesa and off a rim toward a busy road with houses nearby. We cringed at the thought of the crippled buck running through people's yards, and we doggedly kept on him. Several times I just shook my head in disbelief at how Kirt could pick his track out of the hundreds of others we encountered.

Three hours into the tracking job, Kirt made a big loop, backtracking into some stunted Gambel oakbrush. He said the buck was in there and I should get ready. I found a fence post and steadied my rifle on it. A few minutes later, I saw the buck stand up among the oaks. Kirt had no shot, so I took him out.

Kirt was an outfitter for over 40 years and became an excellent tracker. Here is his 180-class public-land buck taken after a long dry tracking job. This buck later lab-aged at 7 years old.

We checked the buck and found that Kirt was right: he had broken the buck's back leg, but that was the only injury. Had we not tracked the buck, he would have become coyote fodder in back of someone's house. I knew then and there that no matter the problems Kirt has had or what people say, he is still one of the best to ever hunt big mule deer.

As we shared Rum and Cokes back at camp, I knew I'd witnessed something few hunters ever will. I also knew it might be the last hunt Kirt and I would share. So far, unfortunately, that has been the case. I love and care about Kirt Darner and know I wouldn't be the buck hunter I am today without his friendship. God knows I'll miss him when he's gone.

I killed a pretty good buck on that same hunt while sneaking through some heavy aspen and Gambel oak, shooting this buck in his bed at 70 paces. This is the only buck in 20 years that the lab hasn't been able to determine an age – because of abnormal tooth growth.

I'll close this section with this thought: A good partner is hard to find. If you find one, plan some hunts together; they may be your most memorable. However, if you really want to be successful at killing big mule deer, you must be prepared to hunt alone; for one reason or another, that will often be the card you're dealt. If you can't hunt alone, you'll miss half your hunts.

THE ONE THING

So I've laid out the mental game of hunting big mule deer: why you must change, why your thinking must change, and why you have to focus.

However, there is one more skill you must develop if you're ever going to take a big mule deer. This skill starts with your thinking.

I know a deer hunter from Idaho who has been very successful on mule deer bucks. He is the hunter everyone envies, as he's always got antlers sticking out of the back of his truck. Rarely does he come home with an unpunched deer tag (or elk, antelope, whatever). He's been killing nice bucks since he was a teenager over 30 years ago. I'd guess he has more than 35 bucks scoring between 150" and 170."

I learn something from most every deer hunter I meet and he's no different. He's a very patient hunter and can spend all day afield in a very small area without getting bored. Most hunters can't do that (including me, some days). About 30 minutes after sunrise they give up and start hiking to the next ridge (meanwhile spreading their scent and noise across the countryside), and they rarely if ever see a really big buck. He's also an excellent shot and will hunt with any weapon. I think he's a better hunter than I am if you consider patience, personality (he's very calm, I'm very hyper), and ability to hunt all day.

One day he stopped by my house to chat about big mule deer. He looked at all my biggest bucks and was perplexed at how "lucky" I've been. He didn't say this in a rude way, but wondered how we both could be hunting some of the same country, yet he'd taken bucks only up to about 170" and many of mine were between 170" and 230."

There is only one thing I do differently than he does. Either by foolishness or just plain stubbornness, I've developed the ability to pass up the nice bucks and on some hunts, even the really good bucks. By doing so, I've still been on the mountain long after everyone is at the skinning pole. By developing this skill, I've had shots at my biggest bucks. This skill is determined by how you think. I "think" that if I plan, scout, hunt hard and smart, and don't just define success by the kill, that I *can* find a bigger buck. I've had this point driven home many times over the decades. We're long due for a buck story and the following should illustrate what I'm talking about.

WYOMING NON-TYPICAL

When the fog thinned enough that I could see again, there were two bucks standing amongst the thick spruce. The 30" typical was still facing me at 80 yards, but behind him was a second deer. Keeping my eye to the scope, I could see that he also spread 30 inches but had much more mass and plenty of extra points. His main beams were long and nearly as high as his tall back forks. I was sure he was the buck I'd been after. I felt a tightening in my gut as I fought back the buck fever. If only he'd step out from behind the other buck!

This wasn't the first time I had seen the typical buck since I'd started hunting the non-typical in early September. I'd spent nearly 16 days over the last month waiting for a chance at the giant. I'd had several, but he'd always given me the slip. I had seen the typical buck at least five other days, and each time I reluctantly passed him up for the remote chance at the bigger deer if I could find him. The typical was a beautiful buck with long sweeping beams and back forks that laid out well, giving him his wide spread. He'd gross near 190" and on most hunts, I'd be very happy with him. However, the non-typical was a much bigger deer and would easily break 220." Like all really big deer, he was smart as a fox, and I rarely could find him on the huge mountain he lived on. If the wind didn't change, I might finally have my chance at him.

After a minute or so of staring through my scope, the bigger deer turned his head to the left, revealing even more extra points, but my shot was still blocked by the typical. I held steady, safety off, finger on the trigger. They were getting nervous, they knew my dark form shadowed in the timber might be danger. The non-typical took a nervous step to his left, barely exposing his chest from behind the other buck.

I don't remember pressuring the trigger, only the awesome sight of the two big deer in my scope as the rifle recoiled. The biggest buck staggered and then spun around, disappearing into the spruce. The typical craned his neck out toward me in surprise, because he'd had a bullet whiz just a few inches past his left shoulder. He quickly whirled and followed the other buck into the spruce and down the steep slope.

The Speer bullet had done its job. I found the non-typical on his back with his antlers buried deep in the snow 100 yards down the mountain. I thanked the Lord for this life He'd just given me and sat down beside the animal. His crimson blood stained the snow.

As I rolled him over I felt my heart racing. His light-colored antlers were heavy, his main points even. His Boone and Crockett typical frame carried nearly 20" of extras. I was sure the 9x7 antlers would gross at least 220." As I beheld his spectacular antlers, my mind wandered back over the days I'd hunted him. While scouting, glassing, and tracking were all important skills in taking him, none of them superseded my ability to pass up the other buck.

I passed up a 30″ 190 Gross buck five times over the course
of a month just for a chance at this buster. I've killed
some of my best bucks in blizzard conditions.

I'm often asked if there's a secret to killing a big mule deer. While a hunter must be skilled at glassing, tracking, still hunting, ambush hunting, and identifying likely buck country, none of these abilities will guarantee anyone a truly big deer. There's only one sure-fire skill a guy can count on for a chance at a big buck: the ability to pass up the smaller bucks.

If a hunter can learn to pass up bucks that don't make the grade, I can virtually guarantee he'll eventually have a shot at a big buck. Almost sounds too simple, doesn't it? Yet I've seen more good tags go to waste, including my own, because hunters can't pass on those other smaller deer.

THE PHYSICAL

A S MULE DEER HUNTING HAS BECOME TOUGHER in many areas, many hunters have figured out that the beer belly and bacon cheeseburgers don't mix with hard-core buck hunting. An entire subculture of physically fit hunters has emerged in the last decade. Good for us, I say. The antis often paint us out to be Bubba – 80 pounds overweight and not capable of doing anything more physical than riding an ATV. Well, I guess they could be right about some hunters, but less so now than in the recent past. Many hunters are training six days a week, running marathons, and even entering competitions geared toward hunters. Hunters including Cameron Hanes, Aron Snyder, and David Long take fitness for hunting to the max, and their hunting successes mirror their physical fitness.

If you want to be inspired physically, follow these men on social media – skipping a workout will make you feel as guilty as sleeping in on opening morning.

I haven't mentioned it yet, but I've made my primary living as a personal trainer for 23 years. Physical fitness ranks high in my life and in the field.

I currently manage a large staff of personal trainers serving thousands of clients per year. To my knowledge, we operate the largest training program in Idaho. The club I work in has 1,500-2,000 member visits *per day*. Based on this experience, and what I see going on in the hunting industry, I'd like to offer my thoughts on where fitness fits in for the big mule deer hunter. Mind you, this subject would take an entire book to cover properly, so I'm just giving you some general direction here, not a program!

First, I'm no fitness icon myself. Of course I maintain year-round fitness and keep a decent body weight, rarely fluctuating more than about seven pounds a year. I can lift my body weight in all the major lifts like squats and benchpress and pull-ups, and maintain a V02 Max (a measure of cardio-respiratory fitness) of around 15-16 METS (competitive athletes like marathon runners are closer to 20 METS with world-class athletes pushing 30 METS.) My body fat varies between 14 and 18 percent. However, compared with the really athletic hunters I know, I'm kind of a pud. These guys can run ultra-marathons, carry 110-pound packs, and maintain less than 10 percent body fat year round. If I tried to out-climb them, I'd be eating dust as I watched their Vibrams fade in the distance. Luckily, you don't have to be ultra-fit to succeed at big buck hunting. In fact, if you're only fit and nothing else, you won't kill many big mule deer because you'll hike right past them.

TRAINING SPECIFICITY

In the training world, there is what is called the principle of specificity, the principle of training that states training should be relevant and appropriate to the sport for which the individual is training. In the training world, the principle of specificity is like the law of gravity – it's true whether you believe it or not. However, I notice that many hunters don't apply the principle correctly.

Big buck hunting in rough terrain is mostly an anaerobic sport, meaning short bursts of high-intensity exercise (climbing) with short rests. The gentler the terrain, the more you rely on aerobic conditioning, which allows you to produce less effort but over much longer duration. I think most mule deer hunting is a mix of aerobic and anaerobic fitness. You don't want to be only aerobically fit or only anaerobically fit, but rather a balance of the two, to hunt well in typical mule deer country. Running, especially marathon running, is purely an aerobic sport, save maybe the last few minutes if the runner is sprinting for the finish line. On the same note, lifting weights to produce muscle hypertrophy (an increase in number or size of muscle fibers) and strength (an increase in muscle fiber efficiency) is an anaerobic exercise.

Think about it. How often are you actually running while deer hunting? Likewise, having really big biceps doesn't mean you'll be able to backpack 100 pounds of deer meat without tearing up your knees or your back.

Applying the principle of specificity, I advocate a training program that mimics what hunters do, incorporating a balance of aerobic (cardio-based) exercise and anaerobic (resistance-based) exercises. The program needs to be periodized, i.e. broken down into cycles that manipulate training type, volume, intensity, and other variables so you reach your "peak" conditioning at the same time your event is scheduled (hunting season in our case.)

I incorporate many exercises that develop strength,
endurance, balance, and quickness.

A properly designed program goes way beyond the "No Pain, No Gain" mantra that dominates most gyms (and which I would argue produces way too many injuries). It is the smart way to train that will maximize performance with the least time and effort required and lower your rate of injury to almost nil. I'm surrounded by 18-60-year-old guys in great shape, and way too many of them are injured from improper training (often too intense with not enough recovery). I've known some of these guys for 25 years and have seen firsthand that while bad training might make you look good, you'll be old before your time. I've been training since I was 16 and have never had a significant injury resulting from exercise. Again, I'm not a fitness superstar, but I'm not torn up from the floor up either. I'd like to hunt deer until I'm 80 (my grandpa hunted until he was 75), but if my joints are thrashed and my axial skeleton (the spine/pelvis – the foundation of the body) isn't functioning properly, I'll be done before I'm 60.

Again, this subject would take another book to cover completely, so I advise spending some money and time with trainers with plenty of experience training athletes. If you can find a trainer certified by the National Strength and Conditioning Association who has more than 5,000 client-hours, hire that guy and listen close! If you can't find one, email me at my day job at robby@appleathleticclub.com – I have two on my staff and can phone consult for a fee (and it ain't cheap).

Pilates isn't just for girls! Besides alleviating back pain,
Pilates can prevent many injuries incurred both in and out of the gym.

As far as my own program, once per week I do the modified Olympic-style lifts like squats, power-cleans, push-presses, and snatches, along with chest/shoulder presses and back rows in the 6-12 repetition range. Two days of the week I do super-circuit weight training (45 seconds of weights in 12-15 rep range, 15-second break, 45 seconds cardio at 70-90 percent max heart rate). I do pure cardio exercises (run, various cardio machines) in the 70-90 percent of max heart rate range 3-5 days per week. I also do sprints. Twice weekly, I do Pilates-based core training to protect my back. I include flexibility training on most days. Because my program is periodized, the type, volume, and intensity of these exercises vary. For example, as I get closer to hunting season, my intensity increases but my volume drops.

NUTRITION FOR HUNTING AND LIFE

Just as important as your physical routine is your diet. With 70-80 percent of Americans overweight (looking around, hunters aren't faring much better), it's safe to say that what most people are doing isn't working. Also, heart disease and cancer are the leading causes of death in America but can largely be reduced by proper diets rich in whole minimally processed foods.

I'm completely jaded against the fad diets that get so much press – like Paleo, Atkins, and the dozen or so spin-offs you can find on bookshelves any given year. Why? Two reasons: One because I witness at work daily how many people fail in the long run and two, because for most people these meat and vegetable diets aren't sustainable for more than a few months, leading to high drop-out rates. Most of the hype you read on the internet is from the honeymooners (been on the diets less than a year), or the really hard-cores who think everyone can just man up and eat like they do. Few people chime in on forums after they've gained all the weight back, so the average reader is left thinking everyone is doing great on these programs. If you can handle eating the way these diets coach *for the rest of your life*, go for it. A *few* people can handle it, and I'd never argue against their success.

However, the average hunter is trying to swing a mortgage, take care of a family, and hold down at least one job along with all the typical stressors life throws at him every day. His family, not some professional sports team, owns his body. This hectic lifestyle makes it very hard for a person to stick to a strict diet plan. This guy needs to know how to choose from a wide variety of foods if he's going to succeed. Just last week I bought a friend lunch, a guy who's been on one of these strict diets for a few months. It took five minutes just to figure out which restaurant we could eat at, and five more for him to pick the croutons out of the salads we both ordered because he won't eat grains. The chances of him sticking with his program more than six months are dismal, no matter how much weight he loses in the short term.

I advocate good old calorie counting in a food journal or online application like My Fitness Pal. Despite what the naysayers say, a calorie is still pretty much a calorie (a few small hair-splitting differences might exist). People who dispute this are left with eating a relatively small number of foods and have little variety (the spice of life) in their menus, leading to high drop-out rates. By learning about how much you're really eating (if you're overweight, it's way more than you think), then learning to make better choices from a wide variety of food (not just a list of 20 foods like the diets throw at you), only then can you be successful in the long run. In the game of weight loss and weight maintenance, it does no good to lose 25 pounds and then gain it back; the tortoise wins the race. The hare makes headlines with the 50-pound loss but is soon gaining it back along with the shame and poor self-attitude the failure brings with it. Soon he's back to the junk because that is all he understands after wasting six months doing something virtually no American can do long term.

Choose a diet that is primarily made up of whole, minimally processed foods from lean proteins (including dairy), whole grains (notice I said WHOLE), fruits and vegetables, mostly healthy fats (the plant-based fats), and about 0.5 to 0.75 ounces of water per pound of body weight. Limit unhealthy choices (foods high in sugar and fat) to 10 percent or less of your daily calories. None of this is earth-shattering or exciting and is why it doesn't sell many books, but it works in the long run. Like the exercise, this too, would take another book to cover properly. If you're interested in learning more, you can contact my staff of trainers through robby@appleathleticclub.com or search for the "Diet" thread on the forums at rokslide.com – the thread has been "hit" nearly 20,000 times since I wrote it in 2012 and I continue to get emails from members seeing success from what they learned.

In the end, you have to be fit enough to hunt without getting too sore or fatigued or plain old hurt during your hunt. You need to apply year-round discipline to staying in a routine that works for you. Don't be the guy who starts working out 30 days before the hunt going full-bore and then quitting once the hunt is over. It's better to work out three times per week year-round than try to make it all up a few weeks before the hunt. If you can stay in decent shape year-round and then train five to six days per week starting 90 days before season, you'll do way better on the mountain and get the most out of your hunt. Year-round fitness feels great and you'll likely live a lot longer, which means way more big bucks on the game pole.

PART III: JUDGING BIG MULE DEER

I N MY DEFINITION OF BIG mule deer, I mentioned age, body size, and antlers. It's mostly body size and antlers you'll be judging in the field; however, I can tell in the field whether a buck is older than four, with good accuracy, and so could you with practice. For this section, I'm writing primarily about antler size, as that is how most of us will make the decision to pull the trigger.

Ground shrinkage is a term widely used among hunters to describe the phenomenon that occurs between the moment a hunter pulls the trigger and when he walks up on his fallen "trophy." Oftentimes the buck's antlers are six inches narrower and score 20" less than what the hunter thought they would. This has happened to me on occasion, too. Ground shrinkage occurs when we can't accurately judge the size of a buck and his antlers (and buck fever doesn't help). There are solutions to make sure you don't encounter ground shrinkage when you finally wrap your hands around those long-sought-after antlers.

GROSS BOONE AND CROCKETT SCORE – THE PREFERRED DIY SYSTEM

If you want to shoot a truly big deer that scores well, you need to learn the Boone and Crockett system. While I might list score last in my definition of a big mule deer, it's still very important and is how most of us judge a big deer. I recommend learning Boone and Crockett's system because it is the most widely known and accepted (plus B&C is a great conservation organization). Some argue that others like Safari Club International or the Burkett system are better. While I can't argue which system is the best, I use Boone and Crockett's. It is so well known that most hunters talk about score without ever mentioning Boone and Crockett. They say something like "Fred killed a 180 buck up on Tater Hill last week," and most hunters automatically know they mean Boone and Crockett gross.

If you don't understand how to score a mule deer, you can check out boone-crockett.org and look for the link to Field Judging North American Big Game. There are some excellent tools there that will serve you much better than I could here.

I've judged bucks in the field for nearly 30 years and while I can get net score with a good look and a few minutes to run the math, I've learned that big bucks can be judged more simply by calculating gross.

Once you've learned Boone and Crockett's system, to arrive at gross score, simply add up all the inches of points, beams, and mass measurements, throw in the inside spread and any extra points, and you've got gross score. Most hunters think gross score most fairly awards a buck for the amount of antler he grew, while net penalizes most bucks. I think net is great for keeping record books, but gross is more practical to use afield.

If I've got time to accurately judge a buck afield, the conversation in my head will go something like this:

18" backs so 36 there,

11" and 10" G-3s, so 21 + 36 is 57,

10" G-4s so 20 + 57 is 77,

add 5" for brow tines and 72" for main beam/inside spread to get 154

add 34" for mass and I'm at 188

plus 10" of stickers puts that buck at 198" gross – bang!

Truth be told, though, a buck with a 198 gross score looks "Big" and I just get ready to kill him without worry of score. That is why score is listed last in my definition of "big." I think we all overplay it and only after hunting DIY a few decades do we realize that we don't need to rely on it so much. You will shoot a big buck most of the time you see one if you consider all the other factors –antler diameter, spread, extra points, and body size – and you should unless you have a very special tag or have scouted a larger buck.

If I hear someone mention a 180" buck, I know that he means 180 gross Boone and Crockett. It doesn't matter if it's a typical or a non-typical, all the inches are included in the score by most hunters. To me, this is the easiest and most practical way to judge a buck anyway. The purists balk at my method but there are so few record-book bucks killed each year, I think we're splitting hairs to worry about it. I'm a DIY hunter and this book is written with other DIY hunters in mind. I know that nearly 100 percent of us won't pass up a big buck just because he's a few inches short of the record book, save maybe the once-in-five-lifetimes draw tags where there is a legitimate chance of killing a book buck if you hold out for one. One Boone and Crockett official measurer I know in southeast Idaho – some of the West's best book buck country – told me that he measures lots of bucks that net in the 180s but rarely one that exceeds 190" (the net minimum for all-time book). That is why my definition of big mule deer only partially considers score – I leave out too many good bucks most hunters would be thrilled to have if I focus only on score.

A buck with about 34 inches of mass.

If you draw that great tag where a record buck is a real possibility, you'll still need to understand gross score to arrive at the net score. If I'm judging a record-book buck, I generally just double the measurements of the shortest points/beam and can get really close, especially with a typical buck.

One trick I learned to speed up the judging process is to use the number 34 when calculating the inches of mass or "H" measurements. Most big bucks are going to be very close to that number unless they are noticeably light or heavy antlered. Mass makes up only 18 percent of the score, and it's even harder to judge than length, so using 34 gets me pretty close.

A buck with 34" of mass will have about 5" H-1 (bases,) 4½" H-2 (between brow tine and G-2,) 4" H-3 (between beam and fork of G-2/G-3), and 3½" H-4 (between G-2 and G-4.) Again that can be hard to judge, but look at a few bucks with 34" of mass and you'll start to get a feel for the minimum that a buck needs.

One measurement, the inside spread, isn't really measuring actual inches of antler, but air between the main beams. That's fine with me, as a buck with a wide inside spread (lots of air) looks bigger than a buck with a narrower but symmetrical inside spread (which is rewarded in the net score.)

This is what a buck with 40" of mass looks like. This buck won me
three rifles in various big buck contests. That's my dad and
my stepbrother Casey with me.

Because I don't rely heavily on record book score when deciding if a buck makes the grade, then what is my definition of a *really* big buck when considering score only? That's an easy one. After observing thousands of big bucks over my hunting career, I think 200 gross inches is a great benchmark for the DIY hunter to achieve.

Any buck with 200" of bone protruding from his head is going to get your blood pressure way beyond what your doctor recommends! A DIY hunter should be satisfied with a buck of that caliber (unless he's drawn the top one or two units in the West or has scouted a 230" buck.) As of press time, I've killed four over 200." See my "Breaking 200" article on rokslide.com for all the stats on those bucks.

A 200" gross Boone and Crockett buck is a lofty but attainable goal for any DIY hunter who puts his mind to the task. I've taken four in the last 18 years and see one about every three years.

PRACTICE MAKES PROFICIENT

You don't have to become an expert at scoring bucks, you just have to become proficient. I'm certainly not great at it. To improve your judging skills, you should practice measuring bucks other hunters have taken. After I measured about five racks, I got a good feel for judging bucks on the hoof. If you know of a buck that has been officially scored, ask the hunter if you can slap a tape on the antlers. I've done this many times and it's really helped me learn to judge bucks more accurately, in both gross and net score. Most hunters are thrilled to meet someone who is excited about their bucks. I've been invited into many a stranger's home simply because I expressed interest in his accomplishments.

If I don't yet know the official score, I ask the hunter not to tell me and see how close I can get my measurements to agree. This is great practice and will be well worth the effort when you're trying to judge a buck in the field.

You should also view as many bucks on the hoof as possible throughout the year. Also, keep in mind that more often than not, you'll over-judge a buck, so keep a little deduction factor in mind. I figure most bucks I judge are at least 5 percent smaller than I think, and I'm usually right if I actually get to put a tape on them.

Thanks to the many videographers whose work has brought some of the finest bucks on earth to our television screens, even unskilled hunters can get a good feel for what a big buck looks like afield. Videographers such as Steve Alderman of Idaho and Ryan Hatch of Utah have given us a mountain of video to enjoy and to learn from. Learning to judge bucks from video rather than pictures is the best. Video gives you a "3-D" representation; you can see many angles of the buck's antlers (and body) compared with a photo, which is 2-D and usually makes bucks appear bigger than they are. I can't explain why, but it seems to be true.

High quality video of big bucks is a resource that wasn't available to the trophy hunters of yesteryear. They had to look at grainy pictures and make their mistakes in the field to improve their judging skills. We've got it easier and it's a good thing, as we don't have the luxury of hunting prime areas year after year like hunters of the past. We often get only one shot at a really good tag, and we'd best be prepared to accurately judge a buck's size.

Whether you're watching videos or actual bucks, you must learn to accurately judge a buck's body size if you hope to nail down a close width or score on his antlers. Compare a buck's body to other deer he's with, or if he's alone, with deer you've seen. A big buck will be about twice as big as a mature doe. The best way to tell this is by his height, which will be about 20 percent taller at the shoulder. When compared with other bucks, a big deer will be heavier-looking in the body, with a noticeably broader chest. Although his head is bigger, his nose will appear shorter and his eyes smaller than those of his buddies.

Most guys know a buck's tip-to-tip ear measurement is around 24" but few realize that measurement can vary from 20" to even 27." A buck with a 20" ear spread and 24" antlers will look like a 30-incher to you if you'd guessed he had a 26" ear spread. All other measurements such as tine length and rack height will look proportionately different as well. You must look at enough deer so you know what a big buck's body looks like compared with other deer. Forsake this practice and you'll be grudgingly tying your tag on a lesser deer this fall.

Know your area's potential.

If you've drawn a good tag, the potential for a big deer should be better, but unless you know for sure the size of bucks in the area, you'll have a hard time passing up lesser deer. To best be able to pass up smaller bucks anywhere, you should scout to see first-hand the size of bucks in the unit. If I've seen a 190" buck in an area, it's easier to pass up a 170-incher that would be dwarfed by the larger deer. If I'm hunting an area for the first time, though, I'm hesitant to pass up nice bucks even though there may be much better bucks available. Only by scouting can I be confident at passing up bucks.

If you just can't scout, or you don't see any really good bucks, rely on your research and what other hunters have taken there recently. Your standards can be only as high as the area's potential where you're hunting. Lesser bucks in one unit can be great bucks in another.

PART IV: FINDING GOOD PLACES TO KILL BIG MULE DEER

I get asked far more "where" to kill a big deer than I ever get asked "how." Many amateur mule deer hunters think they haven't killed any big bucks because they're hunting in the wrong places. While that can be true, I learned early on that you can be hunting all the right places and still not kill a big deer – or even see one. You have to hunt smart and hard in the right places to kill big deer.

Most of this book is dedicated to the "how" and not the "where." There are several reasons. First, if I only tell you where, then I'm not really helping you much. The "where" changes frequently depending on factors including management, drought, hard winters, predators, and disease. You have to learn *how* to hunt first, and then the where becomes more important. It's like the old proverb, "Give a man a fish and he'll eat for a day, teach him to fish and he'll eat for a lifetime."

The second reason is that the "where" isn't that hard to find out anymore. Boone and Crockett has been publishing for decades where record-class bucks have been taken. There are quality research services out there that publish good "where" information monthly. This is information that wasn't available on a wide-scale basis just 15 years ago. As far as where to seek licenses and tags, that's old news now. You're better off spending time scouting and learning good areas than looking for them.

But I do agree that the "where" is very important, and I go to great lengths every year to make sure I'm hunting where my chances are the best at killing a big mule deer. I'll share how I find good places to hunt big mule deer. Before I do, there are a few steps you need take before you start your research.

SET YOUR GOALS

I have to know what I want before I start. To me, I want a buck four years or older with a 180" gross Boone and Crockett score or other features like a wide spread, heavy antlers or some combination of each. To maximize size in the antlers department, I'll likely need to hunt units that have traditionally produced record-book bucks according to the Boone and Crockett all-time record books. This is not a hard-and-fast rule, as some amazing bucks show up in counties that aren't well represented in the record books, but as a starting point, I'm looking for areas with the best genetics. If you're not so picky, you'll have better draw odds than I will.

I also want a quality experience, meaning some country where I can apply the skills I've earned relying less on luck and more on skill. I likely won't be alone, but I also can't be hunting in a pumpkin patch with hunters on every ridge (few if any big bucks live in those places). I also want to be able to hunt the area multiple days yearly, preferably 7-20 days, as that is what it seems to take to kill a smacker buck.

Finally, if I can hunt the area more than once every few years, that is a big plus. It is very hard to learn enough about an area in one season to be successful. Don't let the stories in the magazines fool you. Just because someone showed up for the first time and killed a giant buck in a unit doesn't mean that is the norm. It is the exception (but makes for great stories). So if I find an area I can continue to hunt on a regular basis, my odds go up. For example, I hunted western Wyoming about nine years before I killed a buck that broke 200." It took that long to learn the country and find a buck of that quality. Had I drawn Wyoming's best unit but could hunt it only once (very common for the best units anywhere), I doubt I could've killed a 200" deer my first year.

With those goals in mind, I'm looking for an area that historically grows big-antlered deer, limits hunter pressure either by remoteness, limited tag numbers, private property, or low deer numbers (or some combination of these), and allows me to hunt the area every few years.

SET YOUR BUDGET

"Where should I hunt?" is one of the most frequent questions I am asked, yet I find few of these hunters have set their budget for money and time. By doing this, the question of "where" will almost answer itself. I used to plan hunts with no regard to budget. That killed my bank account and just as bad, had me hunting units where I logistically wasn't efficient, wasting more money and time.

When it comes to money, realize that hunting is expensive but hunting for big mule deer even more so. Besides the great gear it takes, you also have to invest in travel and time away from income-earning activities. I've been hunting out-of-state on my own dime since I was in my early twenties. I've always had a second (and third, and fourth) job to make sure I had the funds to hunt where and when I wanted. I've taken hundreds of days off work "unpaid," so my income had to make up for that somewhere, too.

Many hunters don't realize how much it costs to hunt far from home. The AAA and the IRS both put cost-per-mile near 60 cents. Considering that most of us need a truck to hunt, we're going to be even higher. If your hunting area is 600 miles away, you'll spend a minimum of $720 per trip. As I recommend pre-scouting any new area, those figures double! That cost is fine if it fits your budget and the unit gives you a better chance than something closer to home.

The cost of tags is pretty reasonable if you're lucky enough to be able to access big mule deer in your own state, but if you start applying out of state, your tag and application fees climb fast. The last three years, my tag/application fees have averaged $1371 and I've hunted only two states each of those years. I don't borrow money or use credit cards anymore, so my budget is based on cash-on-hand versus the value of the hunts in the areas I'm considering. Knowing what I have to spend really helps me narrow down where to hunt.

Considering time, you need to assess your time budget as you plan your hunts. I think you have to hunt 10-30 days per season (not necessarily consecutively) to kill a big deer, so make sure you schedule that much time. To hunt this much, it's likely something has to give, so be prepared. You simply can't have your cake and eat it too.

You also need to remember that you may draw more tags than you planned, squeezing your wallet and vacation time even more. Some states allow you to turn tags back for a refund or points reinstatement. I've had to do this a few times over the years. However, if you draw several great tags, you're not going to want to turn them back and you need to have enough money and time to hunt them correctly.

By setting your budgets, you can narrow down which hunts make the most sense to apply for or to buy OTC tags.

START YOUR RESEARCH

With clear goals and a time and money budget set, you can start researching where to either buy OTC tags or apply for limited quota tags or both. Your research will fall into two categories: Big Picture Research and Small Picture Research. Big Picture Research means selecting which state, area, and unit best fit your goals and budgets. Small Picture Research is the process of finding the exact country – drainages, ridges, basins, hillsides – where big mule deer live. Many hunters really never get beyond the big picture.

Who says only trophy units are good? This 38″ wide 230 gross buck came out of a central Idaho unit not really known for big bucks. Licenses are OTC and hardly anyone hunts there. Those who do rarely hunt it right, although the guy who shot this bruiser certainly did.

Before I share the resources I use to paint the big picture, there are three very important considerations to ensure your research is effective. Too often there is a serious separation between a hunter's expectations and reality. If you don't understand reality, you'll waste time and money researching areas that won't really increase your success rate on killing big mule deer.

CONSIDER THE MULE DEER COUNTRY CLOSER TO HOME

Too many hunters don't realize the toll on energy, time, and funds that travel will mean. It's too easy to sit at your computer in mid-January and make giant plans to travel the West looking for big mule deer. The reality is that come fall, you're going to be stressed at work and not have the vacation time you'd planned, Jr. will have broken his arm at football practice taxing your cash flow, and your buddy will bail on you at the last moment so he can work on his house. Suddenly that 1,000-mile drive seems about as fun as giving birth to a flaming porcupine. If you do make it to your unit, you're going to feel like a stranger in a strange land and the thought of going home to mama and the kids will pull you like a magnet.

With hunt options closer to home, you can still hunt enough days to kill a big deer even if the unexpected happens – as it often does. Also, hunting closer to home gives you an advantage you won't have anywhere else: the ability to visit the area more often. You'll feel more confident in your abilities when hunting there.

Consider all your options close to home first. It's really easy to get the grass-is-greener syndrome; big deer hunting is tough all over. It's rather foolish to drive through units and states that could meet your goal to get somewhere where you have to overcome the same problems you do closer to home.

I've killed two of my biggest bucks hundreds of miles from home in Colorado, but I've killed two others just as big (bigger actually) very close to home, and a slew of other good bucks within a few hours' drive. Logistically I can spend more time in those areas and consequently end up killing more big deer there than even great units a state or two away. If you get to hunt deer only one week a year, it's going to take decades longer to build the skills needed to kill more big bucks. Only by maximizing your time afield can you gain those skills.

If you don't live in a Western state, I think the idea of hunting closer still applies. I get calls all the time from Texans who want to hunt deer in Idaho. My first response is a question: "Why would you ignore New Mexico and Colorado to hunt Idaho, when those states certainly have areas that hold bucks you'll be happy with?"

"Because half of Texas hunts those states," is their usual reply.

"Well half of Oregon, Washington, and northern California hunt Idaho!" is my response.

Or they tell me they've hunted those states and it wasn't good, or the winterkill was bad, or the outfitter lied, or the mountain lions were thick, or whatever! They'll likely encounter those same problems anywhere and would have been smarter learning a place they can visit more often.

All things being equal, you need to hunt as close to home as possible to improve your odds. Save the extreme drives, lost hunting days, and expense for the really good units that give you a clear advantage.

DECIDE WHETHER NON-RESIDENT STATUS WILL HELP YOUR ODDS

If you live in the West, you need to think hard about expanding your reach to other states. This isn't always necessary to kill big mule deer and if you're not careful, it can become a distraction. Many of us, including me, make the mistake in thinking that everywhere else is better. That is rarely true. Just because you drive across state lines doesn't mean you'll improve your odds. You need to spend your limited hunting days in productive deer country to be successful, rather than driving all over the West in search of big deer nirvana (which doesn't really exist anyway). Make sure your reasons for hunting out-of-state are clear and justified, and truly increase your odds of success. Here are some of mine:

Access Special Hunts. My home state of Idaho hosts very few OTC rifle hunts in record-book buck country during the rut, a prime time to kill big mule deer. By applying beyond state lines, I can hunt the rut (and without conflicting with hunts I have scheduled here.)

Access More Big Bucks. Idaho manages for opportunity with a secondary emphasis on growing big mule deer bucks (and they do a pretty fair job if you ask me). By hunting some units in other states, I can access higher numbers of big bucks.

Extended season dates. If you want to kill more than a few big deer, you have to hunt a lot of days. While I can hunt up to 40 days of open season per year, I certainly can't (and don't want to) hunt it all at once. Hunt 10 days straight for trophy mule deer and then try to turn around and do it again with only a few days' break. Most of the time you'll be so emotionally drained that you won't hunt well and will not enjoy it. By hunting other states, I can spread my hunting days out, giving me the needed rest (and keeping the rest of my life functioning well).

Adventure. I have to admit that piling all my gear in the truck, hooking onto the horse trailer, and heading for new country beyond the horizon is pretty enjoyable. However, I don't want to sacrifice hunting days just to hunt new country, so I have to be smart about where I hunt. I want adventure only if it increases my odds of killing a big deer.

DON'T EXPECT TO FIND "SECRET HONEY HOLES" VIA PHONE OR INTERNET

With the rise of the information age, research has become more centralized and in a way, much easier. Several decades ago, I used to receive statistics and other information directly from biologists and game wardens. I spent many hours on the phone talking to hunters, ordered local newspapers/magazines from areas I was researching, and waited anxiously at the mailbox for my maps. It was enjoyable but took many hours of my time. Now most of that information is at my fingertips through state game agency websites, forums, research services, and other resources including Google Earth. The downside with all the readily available information is that there aren't many secrets to be discovered anymore, at least not big-picture information.

I've operated a successful scouting service – WeScout4u.com – since 1997. This has brought me into contact with thousands of hunters. I'm still surprised when someone needles me for the secret "spot" that no one knows about. That is so 1980s! The information age has leveled the playing field. A hunter in Florida can get the same information as the hunter living in the unit.

In the late '80s early '90s, it was possible to be among the first to learn about an area or unit that held big deer. You could usually enjoy many years of hunting before the word got out, more hunters showed up, and quality declined. Those days are gone but not to fret. You just adapt and keep hunting, and success will follow.

I did an internship toward my degree in the mid-1990s. I worked a day a week in an Idaho Fish and Game office for a spring semester when hunters are actively researching hunts. Every day, I'd hear the biologists on the phone telling hunters virtually the same information as what they'd told the last ten callers. Some of these calls were downright hilarious as hunters pried for secret spots, offered money and trades, and even asked where the biologist hunted! Trust me; he's likely telling you everything he knows. If he does have a secret spot, he's hunting it himself and won't tell anyone.

While everyone might know *where* to kill big deer, the masses don't know *how*, and that is how you can set yourself apart. Remember that you're not likely to find what you're looking for by prying other hunters for info, so be realistic and know that your very best information will come from visiting, scouting, and hunting the unit; however, you still need all the information possible to make good decisions on where to hunt.

BIG PICTURE RESEARCH

W ITH A REALITY-BASED PERSPECTIVE, I'M READY to choose units where I have a chance at getting a license. I call this process "Big Picture Research" because a state, unit, or area is just the big picture. Here are the resources I use to paint the big picture.

STATE GAME DEPARTMENTS

The founders of America had a great vision to allow states to self-govern in many public matters, and wildlife management is one of those matters. If you decide that hunting beyond your state lines is an advantage, you'll see every state has a different approach to management that might give you an advantage. Even if you decide to hunt in-state (assuming you have mule deer,) you need to know how to properly research your own state. I find too many resident hunters don't fully understand even their own state's management enough to research areas where big mule deer hunting is best. The following is how I research the big picture using the various state game departments.

BIOLOGISTS

Big game biologists, or specifically mule deer biologists, are still great resources. If they've been in their position for more than five years, they can go way beyond the rote information the guy in fisheries also knows. Some departments have only young inexperienced biologists on the front line talking to the public. Don't be rude, but try to determine whether you're talking to the most experienced person there. I've been lucky enough to know several career biologists with 30 years of experience. These guys are incredible if you can find one. Even if you can't find the old gray-haired biologist whose retirement party is next week, you'll still learn a lot talking to someone who manages mule deer for a living.

When I call a biologist, I always tell them I'm researching some hunts in his area and ask whether it's a good time to talk. I don't want to bother him at a time he's rushed. I'd rather call back later and catch him in the mood to talk. These guys and gals are often under deadlines, especially in the spring when management strategies are being developed, so be courteous.

During the conversation, if they mention a place to hunt, I note it but also remember that they will likely tell a dozen other hunters the same information. More important, I'm interested in a few numbers and always ask for them. Because I'm looking for older, bigger deer, I'm less concerned about success rates (high success rates usually equates to hunter crowding or low draw odds) and total population (huge bucks can come from low populations of deer). Instead, I always ask two things:

1) Is there is a measure of mature bucks in the harvest?

2) What is the post-hunt buck-to-doe ratio?

Number one is not widely publicized for deer, especially on general seasons. Typically, that number is reserved for horned animals like sheep, but some states do measure it for deer and other antlered animals. In most states, I've found biologists who measure it one way or another. If he knows what it is, he will usually be glad to tell you. It's like a badge of honor to him and he'll be impressed that you're asking something beyond "Where should I apply?"

Looking at mature buck harvest is a backwards way of finding big deer in statistics. Usually, hunters look at population numbers and buck-to-doe ratios, which are measures of what the future may hold. Measuring mature bucks in the harvest is how bear and lion biologists work. Because those predators are hard to count accurately (just like big bucks), those biologists rely on harvest information such as tooth samples, certain body measurements, or weight to predict how many older age class animals are in the herd (hey, I really did see a herd of bears once). Studying a measure of mature bucks in the harvest is the same thing.

If you're seeing a stable trend in antler size in the harvest, then it's safe to assume that will continue if all other things such as weather, access, and hunter numbers remain the same. If that number is higher than in other units, you just might be on to something.

For example, Idaho tracks the percentage of 4-points and 5-points *in the harvest*. I've learned over many years that if you can find an area that has around 40 percent of the harvest as 4-point bucks, the unit will have enough older, mature deer to make it worth a try. As I said, it has to be stable. You can't have 40 percent one year then 20 percent the next year (if conditions are the same), as that might indicate the bucks are being overharvested or it's a weather-dependent hunt. Limited draw hunts in good units will often exceed 80 percent, but I think that is partly because hunters in draw units are pickier. However, you can still watch for the trends.

The second statistic I'm interested in is buck-to-doe ratios. Every state measures these numbers, as they are readily available when counting deer from the air or the ground. With higher ratios, there are just plain more bucks in the population and a better chance they'll reach maturity. However, it doesn't have to be high to produce great bucks.

Idaho manages for a minimum of 15 bucks per 100 does in general seasons. Most of our units exceed that number. I've seen huge bucks in units with as low as 15, but I'd rather hunt where there are 20-35 bucks per 100 does. Keep in mind, though, that the higher the ratio, typically the harder it is to get a tag or access (well-managed private property usually has higher ratios).

Utah manages around 18, while Colorado often measures for 30-40 buck-to-doe ratios, even in units where licenses are easy to obtain (a testament that Colorado is truly the West's mule deer factory). I hunted a Colorado unit this year that posts around 30 bucks per 100 does and had no problem finding big mature bucks.

SIGN UP FOR EMAILS

A good way to stay current on a state's mule deer management is to subscribe to their email notifications. You can be among the first to learn anything that might help your success. Right now, I'm planning to apply for a new hunt that isn't even listed in the magazines yet simply because I subscribe to these services. Also, by subscribing, you can even participate in some states' public meeting process, even as a non-resident. Many states understand the information age and know that inviting people to participate in a public meeting – even remotely – will give them a bigger sample size to draw conclusions from. Every time I "log in" on one of these meetings, I learn something that will help me find my next big mule deer.

FIND THE PILOT

I've met only one biologist who was also a pilot. Most departments hire a pilot to fly the biologist over the winter range (and summer range in some cases) to count deer. These pilots can log hundreds of hours looking over some of the West's best mule deer herds. Those I've met aren't hunters, so they don't really have anything to lose by sharing information. There was one helicopter pilot I met that had flown much of Idaho on deer and elk surveys. I asked him if he'd noticed any certain place that was better than others for really big deer.

"Sure, that country from the interstate to the state line seems to always have the biggest bucks. Not as many bucks as other places we go, but certainly the biggest I've seen."

That's coming from a guy who's looked at thousands of bucks all over the state. Talk about a hot tip! While the country he mentioned covered well over 100 square miles, since he told me that 15 years ago several giant deer have come out of those units, and I have seen and hunted a few myself. Rumor is that Idaho might be offering a new rut hunt in one of the units. Odds are I'll be applying!

Another pilot told me that in one mountain range he flies for the department, he's never seen bigger than an average 4-point. While it may grow bigger deer, I can safely ignore it and focus my limited time on country where some bruisers have been seen. While these pilots can be very hard to find, if you run across one, don't be nosy, pushy, or rude, but ask a few questions and see what happens. You might get lucky.

A biologist gave me this photo of two bucks taken on a mule deer survey. Another biologist showed me some shaky video of a 250" non-typical taken from the air. Just a few seasons later, a hunter killed a buck in the same unit that went over 240".

FORUMS AND OTHER SOCIAL MEDIA

Though they've been around since the late 1980s, forums really took off about 2005. Basically a forum is just a big cocktail party for hunters conducted online in a mostly public format. A good forum allows you to interact with other hunters all around the country. You can really get a feel for a new area, find specifics about where to hunt, plan logistics, and in some cases, hook up with a new hunting buddy. Before I continue, I have a forum story.

By another twist of fate (hand of God more accurately), I became an owner of a large forum in the last few years. Rokslide.com was started by David Long and Aron Snyder (big names in the DIY hunting industry), my current partner Ryan Avery, and a few others along with me in 2012. It was really launched as a sort of online magazine. Aron and David have moved on to other outdoor pursuits, so it's now Ryan and me at the helm.

Rokslide's forums quickly became the staple of the website. It's there that thousands of hunters share information on "everything hunting" and is a testament to how information is gathered and shared in this new era. We designed the site to function as a "friendly" place to connect with other hunters. Unfortunately, many other sites let the members run the place and before long it's gone from a nice party feel to more like a bar full of arguing bullies. Rokslide is different. We've had to ban about 300 people since we started to create the community that we originally envisioned – and I can say that it's worked. Many of the Rokslide members are the most helpful I've seen on the web. Stop by Rokslide.com and check out our forums, articles, and the blog (hosted by yours truly) and see if it's right for you. It's free to join.

Although forums can be very helpful in planning your mule deer hunts, they do have limitations. Because I've been a member of a forum (I still like to stop by Brian Latturner's MonsterMuleys.com) and I own a forum, I can give you a solid perspective and some tips.

By nature, people aren't going to give away the areas they've worked hard to learn. That is okay, as many of us DIY-ers like the challenge of learning an area, but you still may need a leg up on choosing a unit. Here's a tip on interacting in forums. Most forums have what is called a post counter. This is a number displayed near your screen name that shows how many times you've posted on the site. Because forums are really just communities, someone with a low post count might not be considered part of the crowd just yet. Forums aren't as anonymous as you might think, and if it's a good community, members will learn about each other and form bonds. When using forums to look for information on where to hunt, don't just jump on and start asking questions. The members will spot you like a fly in the punchbowl and likely won't be as helpful as they are with someone who's been a participating member of the community. Learn to give before you take. Help others with their questions and offer personal insight on subjects you know well. Only then is it acceptable (and effective) to ask for help yourself.

In 2009 I unexpectedly drew a Montana general deer tag my first time applying. Montana allows rifle rut hunts on their general tag. At the time, it took about three to five years to draw, so I hadn't done a lot of research.

When I received notification, I posted on MonsterMuleys.com (I'd been a participating member for years) this question:

"I drew a Montana general tag and would like to hunt an area that has at least the potential to grow a 200" buck. My research has narrowed the state down to the northwest corner or some of the units in the southern portion of the state."

While I got the typical "there ain't no 200" bucks in Montana you fool" responses, I did get one from a nice fellow who knew of some tough-to-hunt areas where few people ventured that occasionally kicked out 200"+ bucks. He offered to help me if I was ever in the area, and I agreed to do the same if he ever got down my way. Well I don't look gift horses in the mouth and a short few months later I planned a scouting trip to the area and met him for dinner (which I bought).

Before you knew it, we were planning a hunt together for November. On November 23, after six days of hunting, I killed a heavy-antlered buck that later was lab-aged at 6 years old. Besides that, though, the Montana guy and I formed a great friendship and are looking forward to hunting together again one of these days. Trevor Carlson and I have become good friends, and if I'd not met him, I never ever would have killed a big mule deer in a general tag area my very first year on the ground.

The web now allows us to connect with other hunters like never before, and that can give you an advantage in finding good places to hunt – an advantage that no one had just a decade ago. Learn to participate in helpful forums and other social media including Facebook and Twitter, and you might just get as lucky as I did.

VOLUNTEER

If you live in a mule deer state or close to one, you might consider volunteering for the various projects and programs offered by the state game departments and conservation organizations. To my knowledge, every state has one. The Mule Deer Foundation hosts projects where volunteers are needed. Volunteering to work in mule deer country not only helps you learn about good places to hunt, it puts you in direct contact with professionals and hunters who are knowledgeable about mule deer. These same people are usually very passionate about mule deer and you'll learn much that can be applied to your own success.

Here I'm listening for radio collar signals from some collared fawns on a project I volunteered for a few years back. I found a 30" typical buck while working that weekend.

Even though I'm an Idaho native and grew up in some of the best Boone and Crockett deer country in the West, I choose to join Idaho's volunteer program. I signed up in the early '90s. At the time, I was probably thinking I'd be cruising the winter range in a Super Cub counting big bucks, but soon found out the check station was the place for the newbies. I also found out that I was expected to be there during deer season!

I worked out a schedule so I could still hunt and meet my commitments. At the check station, I'd help the biologists collect teeth, take certain measurements, and find out where the deer were killed. While I'm sure some of the hunters lied about where they killed their bucks, some were so excited (or intimidated by the badges), many of them told me exactly where they killed them. I know they were telling the truth because I later scouted and confirmed big bucks lived in the areas they'd mentioned.

Besides giving back to my sport, I also connected with many of the best big game biologists and wardens out there. When they saw I was willing to donate my own time, they were more than helpful when I had questions. One year, one of the game wardens I met, Lou Huddleston, offered to take me on a tour of his area and show me where he'd seen many good bucks both alive and taken by hunters. I was sitting in his pickup before you could say "Big mule deer."

Collaring fawns

Lou took me on his route for a day. Even though I'd hunted in his area, he showed me many places that held big deer that I'd had no clue about. That was 15 years ago and I still haven't scouted all the places he showed me. Just last year, an Idaho hunter killed a huge 230" buck in one of the areas we visited that day. Two years ago a friend showed me a picture of a 200" live desert buck from the same area. I'd say my volunteering paid off in spades!

One of the many fawns I collared. I worked with some top notch Fish and Game personnel on this project and learned a bunch of good buck country. I still haven't got it all scouted!

I stayed with the program about eight years before I started my family and just had to give it up (for now) because of time commitments. However, I look forward to the day when I can start volunteering again.

Some states, like Utah, also have volunteer programs where you can get special hunting privileges if you volunteer a certain amount. You'll have to research the opportunities, but trust me when I say you'll get back more than you give.

RESEARCH SERVICES

Over the last decade or so, a few services have popped up that can actually do a lot of research for you. Some are so good at the big-picture part of the research equation that they cannot be ignored. In fact, I saved writing about them until now as they can provide much of the information I've already written about. Many hunters grumble about these services and say they have ruined the draw odds for good hunts. I'd say the information era ruined the draw odds, and these services are just a symptom of the volume of information that's available to today's hunter.

Some hunters wonder whether these services are worth the cost. Twenty years ago, a big buck hunter was paying $100-$200 monthly in long-distance charges to the phone company to research areas. Now for a tenth of that cost, you can access the same or better information from a good research service. Like information on anything, it's become cheaper than it was just a short few years ago.

As of press time, the Huntin' Fool has an office full of consultants whose full-time job is to find the areas where the best bucks (and bulls, antelope, moose, etc.) are coming from. It is very hard to find out anything that these guys don't already know. They also publish lists of hunters who've recently hunted a unit you're interested in, a resource that is more valuable than you can imagine compared with what I had to do just twenty years ago to get good intel. There are other services out there including goHunt.com and Eastman's MSR section of their magazine.

I'm a happily married dad of three active kids and I hold down about three jobs (I lose count), so it's difficult to make time to learn everything I need to know. As a mule deer hunter, I need to hunt about 25-40 days per year to be successful on big bucks. It takes lots of research and time to find areas worth spending my time and applications. About 10 years ago, I came to the conclusion that research services were worth it and got on the bandwagon. They are certainly worth the money when it comes to painting your big picture.

Check out RokSlide.com to see what's available there.

WESTERN STATES OVERVIEW

A S NO MULE DEER BOOK WOULD BE COMPLETE without a snapshot of current opportunity, I'll share my personal thoughts on the subject while we're still on big picture research. However, keep in mind that mule deer are in flux and the information changes every five to ten years, so you always need to stay current on issues affecting mule deer.

IDAHO

Being born and raised here and still living within about a mile of the house I grew up in, you could say I haven't made it very far in life. That's okay by me, as I still live in some of the West's best mule deer country. For all its downsides – wolves, nonrefundable license, high-priced deer tags, poor draw odds – the Gem State also has lots of upsides: the most backcountry of any Western state, general OTC hunts with good bucks available, draw hunts where everyone has an equal chance, relatively long seasons, a second deer tag, and genetics for big deer second only to Colorado.

Many hunters make a few mistakes when considering Idaho. They hear we have a wolf problem – which we do – and they apply that to the entire state. I'd say most deer herds are not being affected significantly by wolves as of press time. Hunters also hear our success rate is low. It is, but that is by design, as few rifle opportunities exist during the rut compared with states such as Colorado and Montana, where most of the rifle hunts occur close to or in the rut.

In the early 1990s, our Fish and Game Department moved most OTC hunts to October dates, well before the influence of the rut. This did two things:

1) Made the hunting tougher.

2) Increased survival for bucks.

I learned from now-retired Idaho biologist Ted Chu that for hunters, perception is too often reality. What he meant is that if we go deer hunting in October and don't see a good buck, we assume they don't exist. Big mistake guys! When you are hunting October bucks that move little and stay in the cover, you won't see them often, but they are still around. Just look down! Something made those tracks.

For example, between me and the two other guys who scout Idaho for my company, WeScout4u.com, we see 10-20 bucks yearly between 170" and 190" across Idaho, mostly in OTC units. I usually kill or at least have a chance at 180-inch or better bucks yearly somewhere in Idaho.

Another Idaho advantage is its late application deadline of June 5. A Western hunter can play the New Mexico, Nevada, Utah, Colorado (some years) and Montana draws before committing to Idaho. There is no sense in having too many tags. You won't do a good job on any of them if you're spread too thin.

Another unique opportunity Idaho provides is its "Unlimited Hunts." These are hunts that have some advantage over the OTC hunts, whether it's hunting a unit with higher buck-to-doe ratios, rut dates, or archery/muzzleloader only. The term "Unlimited" means if you apply, you will draw. However, the OTC hunters can't hunt those units, so pressure drops. Unlimited hunts are a guaranteed draw, and allow you to apply for a good draw tag as your first choice. Keep in mind, Idaho's late rifle hunts are some of the hardest to draw in the West with odds often below 4 percent.

I've killed most of my good bucks in Idaho, not only because I live here but also because I can hunt every year. As a multi-weapon hunter, I can hunt mule deer from August 15 to December 31. This tips the odds in my favor and is why I think Idaho brings stability to your hunting strategy. You can hunt every year and develop your buck-hunting skills. After all, it is ultimately your skills that make you successful. Idaho will require all you've got in glassing, tracking, still-hunting, and patience.

You need to have a long-term plan for hunting Idaho and if at all possible, you need to scout pre-season. You will likely get skunked the first few trips. You have to learn your country, hunt hard and smart, AND hunt enough days. I hunt an average of 20 days yearly in Idaho and still don't kill a good buck every year. Seasons are long enough that you can hunt a week (about the max for most hunters, considering vacation time and mental energy) and still come back, taking advantage of what you've learned.

If your deer hunting strategy is like an investment portfolio, then Idaho is a good slow growth mutual fund. It needs some time to perform.

Idaho offers incredible mule deer hunting diversity. Here I'm glassing the Boise River breaks on a late season archery hunt after packing in three miles by horseback. Nice hat, eh? I think it was 8 degrees that morning.

UTAH

The Beehive State lies just a hundred miles south of my home, so it's always on my radar, although to date I've had only one buck license there (and saw three pretty darn good bucks on that hunt, including a heavy 33-incher not including cheaters). Utah has incredible genetics for mule deer and is probably in the top two or three places on the continent with the potential to grow giant mule deer. A few decades ago, Utah boasted over a million mule deer licenses sold (not sure that was a good thing). Consequently, Utah has a deeply ingrained mule deer culture which is evidenced by the fact that Brian Latturner's MonsterMuleys.com website, Ryan Hatch's *Muley Crazy* magazine, Rusty Hall's *The Trophy Hunter* magazine, and the research service "The Huntin' Fool" were all born in Utah. I can also say that some of the most serious hunters I've meet in the woods across the West have hailed from Utah. When it's in your blood….

Many units in Utah are thick with Gambel Oak, Piñon, and Juniper – perfect habitat to grow and hide giant bucks. I found a 33" non-typical while scouting this unit but couldn't find him again once the season opened.

Utah has many opportunities for big mule deer, but like Idaho, the best hunts are very difficult to draw. Utah was a pioneer in creating top-end mule deer draw units starting well over 25 years ago. Places including the Paunsaugunt and the Henry Mountains have been managed for decades for giant mule deer, and the plan has met with success, growing some of the biggest bucks in modern times. Antelope Island was closed to hunting for decades but now offers a few buck permits for the giants that roam the island. However, getting a license in any of these places is next to impossible for a DIY hunter, even for primitive weapon hunts.

Utah may start kicking out some bigger mule deer on a statewide basis in the near future as it's recently changed its management plan to manage mule deer herds on an individual basis rather than on a statewide basis. I've learned over the decades that some mule deer herds respond quickly to just a little bit of management and big bucks can show up in just a few years where previously there were hardly any. Other places can be managed intensively and respond slowly or not at all, which will certainly be the case in Utah in some areas.

If you live in or close to Utah, don't get the grass-is-greener syndrome I wrote about earlier, as I'd be willing to bet there are big mule deer living much closer to you than you might think. Just this last fall, I learned of several true giants that have come from some of the newly managed units. Utah has both a bonus point system for the high-quality limited entry hunts and a preference point system for the general hunts. I don't think you're wasting time at least researching what Utah has to offer.

NEW MEXICO

I've never hunted New Mexico but did scout there once. The Enchanted State certainly has big mule deer and the genetics to grow absolute toads. However, outside the few high-quality limited units that post draw odds under 5 percent and the Jicarilla Indian Reservation, which is one of the best places in the West to kill a giant mule deer, I'd rate New Mexico as best for a resident or a hunter living close to its borders.

Like all states, not all the big bucks live in the draw units and the persistent hunter who can scout could turn up some very big bucks. New Mexico recently cut its quota on non-resident mule deer hunters in the limited draw units, so I quit applying. I've got better opportunities closer to home, but you may not. If that is the case, look at New Mexico. Don't overlook the September muzzleloader hunts as that can be a prime time to kill a big buck you've scouted up during the summer. According to some in the know, poaching of big mule deer is so rampant in New Mexico that no matter how well managed, the best bucks will go to the poachers – a very sad state of affairs indeed.

MONTANA

Montana isn't widely known for big bucks, but like all states, a little scouting can up those odds. Montana offers a very liberal general rifle hunt almost statewide that runs into late November, a time when bucks are very vulnerable. I have no problem with people hunting bucks in the rut, which is allowed for all big game species, but when it's allowed on a wide scale with almost no limit to hunting pressure, big bucks will be few and far between.

I live close to Montana so I have scouted and hunted there. I killed a really good buck for Montana my very first hunt up there, but that was because of diligent scouting and knowing someone in the area who would help me. I thoroughly enjoyed hunting in the rut taking my big buck on November 23 as I still-hunted through an area littered with big tracks and rubs. I shot him at about 70 yards as he cruised the timber looking for hot does. He later lab-aged at 6 years old, proof that big bucks really can survive heavy hunting pressure if there is enough cover and terrain to hide in. Even with thousands of licenses sold in the area I was hunting, we saw almost no hunters once we got into the deer country that was several miles from the road.

Because of Montana's liberal license structure and mule deer rut hunts, you have to get way back in the thick and nasty to find big mule deer. Here, Trevor and I are five miles from the truck by sunrise looking for horny head. We found him, too!

The Treasure State also has a few high-quality draw hunts, but the non-resident odds are so terrible, applying is an exercise in futility. A few years after I hunted Montana, they upped the general deer tag to $600 and they started squaring points, so I dropped out. The general deer is just not worth that much considering the size of bucks Montana offers versus what I'm seeing in other states. Also, I didn't have enough points to take advantage of the new square formula. Squaring really helped only non-residents with lots of points, so I just put the money back in my budget and left my points on the table. I have a good friend in Montana who I love to hunt with, so I may return someday if my schedule and budget allow. There is more to hunting than just big antlers. Finding a friend you like to hunt with is a "trophy" itself.

OREGON

If you dig through Boone and Crockett's All-Time Record books, you will notice that some of the biggest non-typicals ever taken have come from the Beaver State. Oregon isn't managed well – you'll hear hunters and guides both say that you can tell when you've crossed the state line into Idaho because the big bucks are suddenly bigger. While the big-buck genetics still exist in the herd, few really big bucks are taken by DIY hunters in Oregon. There are a few draw units that kick out big deer if you can get beyond the nearly impossible non-resident draw odds. Oregon almost seems to have a disdain for DIY non-resident hunters if you look at the opportunity that we are offered there. I'd rank Oregon like I do New Mexico: a decent state for a resident or someone living very close to the best deer country, which is in the eastern half of the state.

For years, I also built points in Oregon. Unfortunately, I never really understood their non-resident cap, which is extremely low at 5 percent. Before draw odds got really bad these last 10 years, I was probably getting my money's worth as their license was around $80. However, with worsening draw odds, a license jump to $140, and Oregon's policy of giving its outfitters the non-resident tags every other year in the units I was interested in, I dropped out.

I even wrote their Game Commission a goodbye letter, which they promptly responded to in an effort to keep me. It was too late. I left 5 points, over $500, and a lot of research on the table, but I've never looked back – simply not enough value for the dollar to keep applying. If I lived in Oregon, I know I could fare better as I could scout, and resident draw odds aren't as bad.

WYOMING

Wyoming is at the top of my list for big deer, even though the potential has declined a lot over the last 10 years. While Wyoming limits non-residents, residents can hunt much of the state on a general tag, so pressure is high. Western Wyoming got hit with two bad winters, 2007-08 and 2010-11. That might sound like a while ago, but mule deer are still hurting. Even with these effects lasting, Wyoming is still a good value to me most years because I live so close – I can be there in about an hour. This allows me to scout and hunt frequently, and is the reason some of my best deer have come from the Cowboy State.

While the high country of western Wyoming gets all the press (and all the pressure), there are still vast reaches of Wyoming real estate that hold good bucks where getting a license is no problem. I know of an absolute giant of a buck that rivals any from the West's top draw units killed just two seasons ago in a general unit by an average guy who'd done his scouting. With the lowest human population in the nation, there is plenty of elbow room for hunters willing to work for a buck. Big mule deer can come from any part of the Cowboy State.

Wyoming started a non-resident preference point system just a few years ago and was one of the last Western states to do so. The top hunts were almost immediately clogged with top point holders who still may never draw a tag in their lifetimes. Wyoming does reserve 25 percent of its licenses in a random draw where licenses are drawn regardless of points. As of press time, the preference point system works well for the decent hunts that are lower in demand, but isn't much good for the really high-demand hunts.

Because I live close and licenses are pretty easy to get, I've been taking good bucks in Wyoming since the early '90s. Even back then I hunted in and around the heavy cover.

COLORADO

I receive more questions on Colorado than any other Western state. Rightly so, Colorado has always held the #1 rank in Boone and Crockett mule deer entries – typical and non-typical – in the world. Although the Centennial State started to slip in the '90s, after limited quota hunting was implemented in 1999, Colorado again secured its rank at the top of the heap. Just last year, a hunter by the name of Brett Ross killed a buck in a non-trophy unit that scored close to 300 Boone and Crockett. Who says mule deer are down for the count?

I first started hunting Colorado in 1993 and have seen and taken some of my best bucks there. While many states struggle to maintain 20 bucks per 100 does, Colorado frequently reports buck-to-doe ratios north of 30, even in units with lots of licenses. The state is simply a mule deer machine.

Add to that Colorado's generous non-resident quota of 35 percent (20 percent in units where residents need 6 points to draw), a true preference point system, affordable application fees, a tag refund policy, transferable landowner tags, and the chance to hunt while building points, you might think it's mule deer heaven come lately.

So with all the hype, should you be hunting there? Well, this goes back to some of my earlier comments about time and budget. If you live close to other mule deer country that holds your goal buck, Colorado may just be a distraction. I've learned to focus on my home state of Idaho, but I look to Colorado for opportunity I can't find closer to home. Colorado probably should be on your list as a place to hunt, but don't be enamored with her reputation. Big deer are earned there, and there aren't any shortcuts. Here are some of the obstacles you must overcome to be successful.

Lots of people (and I don't mean just hunters). Colorado is one of the country's fastest growing states. Everywhere I've hunted in Colorado, I've found it's hard to be alone. If you think packing into a vast wilderness far from roads will mean seclusion, think again. Case in point: I found some bucks summering in a highcountry basin in July one year. When I returned for the hunt in September, no less than 15 tents were set up in the basin and not one was a hunter's! Those bucks had long been spooked out of the area.

Lots of private property issues. Much of the best habitat, especially for the rifle seasons, is on private land. A smart hunter can use this to his advantage, but many are caught off-guard if they haven't thoroughly researched their unit. Because of the Texan influence over many decades, much of the best ground is leased, and a smile and a handshake won't get you anywhere.

Though Colorado is the top state for big mule deer, I scouted and hunted about nine years before taking my first buck over 200" there.

Point creep. Since Colorado began limiting its deer licenses, this phenomenon has turned many units, even some that offer just mediocre hunting, into once-in-a-lifetime-at-best draw hunts. I know of several that used to take just one point to draw and offered good hunting. Now they take nearly 20 points, although the hunting is no better than it ever was. This problem is only going to get worse in the near future. Point banking, tried in 2006, would help, but it would take 3-5 years to work and too many hunters oppose it right now.

Overlapping deer and elk seasons. While you might draw a good deer tag, your hunt will still likely be negatively affected by OTC elk hunters. Colorado hosts the West's biggest elk herd and a mind-boggling number of elk hunters in most units. I've hunted units where I've seen few deer hunters but there were elk camps in every turnout and meadow. A smart hunter learns to work with the elk hunters, but don't be deceived, they do influence the hunt quality.

A highly migratory deer herd. While you might find some great bucks summering in Colorado's high country, unless you possess a muzzleloader, archery, or high-country rifle tag, most of the bucks above 11,000 feet will have moved miles by the time the September and October rifle hunts open. Scouting can be a frustrating endeavor for these bucks, as they just aren't around once the later seasons open.

So all things considered, do I recommend Colorado? Yes. I think if a hunter gives himself 5-10 years, he could take a great buck and possibly several. However, he needs to prepare himself physically and mentally for the challenges listed above.

NEVADA

As the Western hunter has evolved these last 20 years, many have decided a state line is no longer a boundary to success. This has worsened draw odds and Nevada is no exception. I sampled four mule deer hunts from around the state, comparing simple draw odds from 1998 to 2013. The odds of drawing decreased by almost 50 percent! Does this mean a buck hunter shouldn't look at the Silver State? That depends on your personal budget (time and money) and goals.

Nevada is certainly a great state for mule deer hunters. The entire state is on a draw system and it's managed conservatively in most units. With fewer hunters in the field, higher buck-to-doe ratios, and a pretty fair bonus point system, Nevada is certainly an attractive option. You do, however, need to consider the entire cost of drawing a tag and that big deer are hard to kill no matter the state or unit.

Nevada has been touted as having the fairest point system in the West. As long as you lay down about $150 for the license, you will receive a bonus point for the next draw (an extra name-in-the-hat system). For subsequent years, that bonus point will be squared. You also have five choices in Nevada, but you lose all bonus points for drawing any choice, which helps the draw odds. You can receive a tag refund if you can't go, or let them keep your money and get your points back plus earn one for sitting out. Despite these upsides, Nevada is still subject to point creep, and their system is expensive unless you draw in the first few years of applying.

Each year, I talk to lots of hunters sitting on 10+ Nevada points who are very frustrated. When they got in the game, many good deer tags were drawn with that many points, but now 10 is just a start. These hunters have at least $1,600 invested with no end in sight. Even if they do draw, most will not see or kill the size of buck they think their money and time investment warrant. Many folks think that a pile of points will guarantee a certain size of deer. Truth be told, points don't guarantee anything. No matter how well a state is managed, older bucks are hard to kill. You have to scout and hunt smart to kill a good buck. If you live close enough to Nevada to learn the unit well, your odds of getting your money's worth go up substantially.

Nevada is also a good option if you're willing to hunt the earlier rifle and primitive weapon seasons as they are easier (relative term) to draw. With any limited draw, make sure you study the draw odds and pick your units carefully. If you're chasing the premium hunts and don't have 10 or more points, statistically you're in for a long wait and even more expense. Nevada does have a transferable landowner tag system; the tags are typically very expensive but allow you to hunt all the seasons on the unit for deer.

ARIZONA

Some places draw a mule deer hunter like a kid to soda pop. Arizona is that place for me. Per tag issued, nowhere else is producing more giant deer than the country north of the Colorado River; the big ditch, as it's called. I've never hunted Arizona, save a February quail hunt once, but to me, Arizona is the essence of a Southwestern mule deer hunt: juniper, sage, oak, ponderosa, remote deserts, and a chance at a truly giant buck.

Arizona, like Nevada, manages many of its deer herds conservatively. Arizona adopted the "Alternative Deer Management Plan" in 1995. The plan identified units that should be managed to harvest bucks in the range of 3 to 5+ years old. This bold management plan has met success, but with both positive and negative effects.

The positive is that some units are now producing bucks that have not been seen since the heyday of mule deer in the 1950s. A culture of big deer hunters has now arisen and every summer, some of the top outfitters and guides start their search for giant mule deer north of the Colorado River. They kill some of the biggest deer on the continent, with several bucks grossing over 300" just in the last few years. A few hard-working and knowledgeable DIY hunters take some giant bucks, too. The odds are stacked against the DIY hunter, as there are lots of eyes, ears, planes, and trail cameras focused on the best units.

The negative side is draw odds. In several of the units, as a non-resident, there is zero chance of drawing a tag unless you have the maximum points. The Huntin' Fool predicts that it will take around 30 years for a non-resident with even two points less than maximum to enter the pool of applicants who have a chance at drawing, then he still may never draw once in the max pool. Too much demand for too few licenses.

Unless I become a resident of Arizona, I will never experience the premier hunts. However, there are hunts where I do have a chance. I'll have to choose a primitive weapons season or a non-rut hunt – or hunt somewhere south of the Colorado River. But at least I'll get to scratch my itch to hunt the Grand Canyon State. I have no grand visions of strolling into a unit and tipping over a 200" buck in one hunt. Based on the last 25 years of my deer-hunting career, I'm more likely to kill one of those in less popular units I can hunt more often. If you're not a max point holder, you'll be better off to spend your time in other Arizona units that offer big mule deer. Last fall, a hunter killed a giant buck close to the Mexico border in a unit few people pay attention to. Like in all states, big mule deer can fall to any persistent hunter outside of the premium units.

If you're contemplating hunting bucks in Arizona, you'll have to plan and hunt smart. Consider, too, that antler growth in many herds is determined by rainfall and can be affected by 20 percent in a bad year (a 200" buck becomes a 160" buck). With hard work, you could realistically find 180+ bucks in a few years of scouting units where you have a decent chance at a tag. If you are an Arizona resident, you have the opportunity to hunt some of the biggest deer on the planet, although draw odds are still long. Start planning now, help friends who've drawn, and get your deer hunting experience in other states while you wait.

OTHER STATES

Notice I didn't mention Washington, California, the Dakotas, Nebraska, Kansas, Iowa, or Texas, even though they all have mule deer and sometimes kick out incredible bucks – a Nebraska hunter recently killed a buck pushing 240". I don't offer advice on these states simply because I don't know much about them. However, if you live in these states, or have good sources there, don't rule them out for hunting big mule deer. Hunting close to home can often bring the best results and every one of those states has the potential to grow big mule deer in certain places.

BEYOND U.S. BORDERS

Mule deer exist from the Tropic of Cancer in Old Mexico to southern Yukon Territory. If you've got the money and time (or live there), some huge

I told my kids they need to start working summer jobs so the ol' man can go to Mexico.

bucks come from Canada and Mexico. Outfitters are the easiest (and most expensive) route, but due diligence is required.

Canada aggressively manages mule deer in certain places and produces some tremendous bucks. Saskatchewan could be the best place outside of the top U.S. draw units to kill quality bucks, but non-residents are restricted to hunting with native outfitters on native lands, so do your research and open your wallet!

Alberta kicks out some tremendous mule deer yearly, but you'll have to go with an outfitter or hunt with a resident if you're not a resident.

Old Mexico has produced some of the biggest desert mule deer on the continent, but has slipped in the last decade. There are some security issues and their management program is often subject to corruption, so it's not what it used to be.

However, a few top outfitters continue to produce excellent bucks. Just a few weeks ago I held a Mexican typical buck in my hands that grossed close to 218." From what I know about Mexico, you'd better plan on hunting multiple years (sounds like here) if you want to kill a really good buck.

Someday and Lord willin', I'd love to add a big desert mule deer to my collection. I just need my kids to start working good jobs so I can afford to go!

DEVELOP YOUR APPLICATION STRATEGY

N OW THAT YOU HAVE THE BIG PICTURE PAINTED – which states, areas, and units to consider – it's almost time to work on the small picture: where exactly you'll hunt in the unit. Before you start that process, you need to have an application strategy. Hunting more than one state (I've hunted up to three a year) can be confusing, as each state has its own system of license and tag distribution. You have to start a year ahead to make sure you're in good mule deer country come the following fall.

From December through June is the application period for draw tags for the Western states, and you have to have a strategy in place or you'll miss deadlines, end up with conflicting hunts, or not end up with anything at all! You also have to make sure you have some OTC hunts to fall back on in the very likely event you don't draw a good tag.

Develop a personal strategy that puts you in good deer country annually for as many days as possible. That word "personal" is very important. You're not like everyone else nor do you want to be. You live in a certain place and have a certain amount of time and money. Like it or not, that is your starting point. If your neighbor is killing big bucks on expensive landowner tags in New Mexico, but you can't afford to play that game, that doesn't mean you can't be successful. You just have to do it differently.

Develop a strategy that takes advantage of your strengths. If you have ample vacation, you can look all over the West for hunts, or if you're a weekend warrior, focus on areas closer to home. I know one local deer hunter who rarely travels more than 50 miles and kills big deer every year from mountain peaks to the desert floor. Maybe he should be writing this book! I wrote about the importance of focus earlier, and your application strategy must focus on your strengths.

For example, one of my favorite mule deer states recently planned a new high country rifle mule deer hunt in September in some of the West's best giant buck country. I probably have enough points to draw it, but I also know where a 215" non-typical Idaho buck has shown up for the last three seasons during the September archery hunt where a tag is guaranteed. I know the area he calls home very well, but know little about the new hunt other than the general mountain ranges. I have a hunting buddy in the new area who could probably help me. I'm torn between the two hunts and still not sure what I'll decide, but my strength probably lies in hunting the Idaho buck (assuming he survived the winter.) Ahhh, what to do?

My point is that a big mule deer hunter better have an application strategy in mind if he wants to have the best shot at a top-end mule deer. Unlike the '80s, few areas produce them and you have to plan way ahead.

Once you've developed your strategy, you have to treat it like you would an investment portfolio. After all, that's what it is: an investment in your hunting future. Just like an investment portfolio, conditions will change and require you to change your strategies, so you need to stay on top of factors that might change your strategy, like killer winters, new hunts, price increases (or drops – I've seen that happen, too).

As you develop your own strategy, make sure you understand reality when it comes to drawing the really good tags. You simply can't rely on great draw tags to kill big mule deer. They're too hard to draw and even if you do draw, you'll likely be very new to the area and your odds of doing well are pretty slim. Here is the reality of today's draw odds and a glimmer of hope if you just can't draw.

DECLINING DRAW ODDS

The draw odds for quality tags have worsened significantly with the rise of the information age. I did a comparison of four of Idaho's muley draw hunts, two high-quality units and two quality units. I looked at the total licenses, applications, and draw odds percentage in 1999 versus 2014. It's a sad story to say the least:

In 1999 there were 400 tags available, 3,286 applicants, and 12 percent draw odds.

Fast forward to 2014 and 330 tags were available, 5,546 applicants applied, and 6 percent of hunters drew.

While odds have always been low, they are dismal now. You will see very similar trends across the West for all good mule deer hunts. It's for this reason that a hunter wanting to take quality bucks cannot count on draw tags. Even with the various versions of point systems across the West, most will agree that they have not solved the problem of increasing demand; there are just too many of us wanting to hunt a few units. A wise hunter needs to view the high-quality Western draws as part of his application strategy, not the focus of it.

I started playing the draws for mule deer in the early 1980s in my home state of Idaho. By 1991 I was applying for tags across the West. At one point, I was applying in nine Western states. I tracked every dollar I spent and by 2010 decided that the return on investment was falling faster than my draw odds were improving.

I also noted that in 25-plus years of applying, I'd drawn only one high-quality tag. I'd scouted the unit relentlessly and did kill a great buck, but during those decades, I'd also killed numerous good-to-great bucks on easy-to-obtain tags across the West in units I'd learned to hunt right. It was clear that my odds of killing a great deer were better in the easier-to-get units. That realization changed everything.

My son Cash holds the antlers of a big Colorado buck from a good draw unit.

I'm currently applying in six Western states after dropping Montana, New Mexico, and Oregon because of the poor value per dollar spent. If my funds were not limited by budget, I may have stayed in, but really wouldn't expect a high-quality tag in my lifetime from those states. I'm now trying to focus on the units I've learned over the decades where I have a chance to hunt most years, even if it means switching weapons. An often-ignored key to killing great bucks is being persistent enough to hunt a unit a few years, even when you're not successful. You can do that only in units you can get a tag in at least every few years.

My application strategy has become like a well-diversified investment portfolio. I have a mix of applications in high-demand units in Arizona, Utah, and Nevada, but also apply for hunts I'll likely draw every other year in Wyoming and Colorado and Idaho. Finally, I hunt Idaho's general seasons every year. I'll also buy landowner tags on occasion, and have never paid more than $1000 for one.

I spend 35-60 days per year scouting and hunting mule deer. That is my "secret" strategy if one exists, and one reason I choose to hunt only deer. If I maximize my time in units that have some good bucks – and many in every Western state still do – I'll eventually get the drop on one. It's happened dozens of times and will happen again – Lord willin' of course. It will happen for you, too, if you play your cards right.

SMALL PICTURE RESEARCH

TALKING TO BIOLOGISTS, LOOKING AT STATISTICS, AND visiting forums are all great and necessary, but can tend to cause a hunter to think too big. We need more specific information.

Our research often causes us to think in units, but quality bucks think in terms of habitat and security. We often mistakenly show up for the hunt expecting the reputation of the unit to produce the results. In reality, we need to find *exact places in the unit where the bucks are living* and hunt those places correctly for the best results. I call this part of the process the "small picture." Most hunters stop at the big picture and then wonder why they didn't kill a big mule deer even after hunting hard for days on end.

Usually, the best source of information is going to come from your own scouting and hunting. Typically, you'll need to narrow down a big unit to smaller bites of country where you can focus your hunting days. That takes time – often several seasons – and is where you can get ahead of other hunters who are thinking too big and jumping around too much.

A unit may be draw or general – the bucks don't care – but usually has small pockets of protection you can find by scouting and hunting. Learning the two ridges and basin where a buck lives is virtually impossible unless you are there and there repeatedly. This is thinking small but produces the best results.

By thinking too big, we sometimes rule out units that have the potential to meet our goal. "Unit X isn't good for big bucks" can be an over-generalization. The unit may not be considered good, but parts of it could still produce great bucks.

For example, some units have low success rates for big deer, so hunters look elsewhere. Well, "elsewhere" might have a higher success rate, but will also attract more hunters and likely carry a younger age class of bucks (unless it is a low-odds draw tag). By thinking smaller, we might consider units that are often overlooked in the statistics. You have to scout to find these units, but they are out there.

A friend of mine found a tenacious buck a few years back in a unit that butts up against a fairly big town in southern Idaho. Most people think of the unit as a place to kill a meat buck, and for the most part, it is. However, my friend is a great buck hunter and looks for the small parts of units where bucks find the needed security and feed to survive and thrive.

One August morning, he found this buck – a buck over 30" wide – living a mile from town in some rough coulees that for the most part held very few deer. It was definitely not a destination for trophy hunters and the unit would never be listed in the latest magazines as a must-apply.

I try to scout places like that when possible. Often I come up empty-handed, but on occasion, I'll find a real sweet spot that's been overlooked because of the unit's average reputation.

The photo shows a relatively small mountain in a unit that produces low-to-average stats on deer and big deer, yet I've seen several of the best bucks of my life there. I found it by visiting the area, talking to locals, and getting my boots on the ground. Make sure in your research that you get beyond the big picture.

The reason I talk about focus so much is that if you're not focusing almost year-round on finding big mule deer, you'll be in the same boat as thousands of hunters come opening day. Those hunters will be in good units with plenty of good bucks within rifle reach, yet well over 90 percent of the hunters will go home with a little buck or nothing at all. They didn't know where and how to hunt the bucks in the particular place they've chosen. Even when you do know exactly where to hunt, big mule deer are tough to kill – but knowing the area one or more of them call home will keep you out there day after day until it eventually happens.

I've run a successful scouting business since 1997 and have put hundreds of hunters in country where I've seen bucks they'd be more than happy with, including a few really big bucks. Some have killed some great bucks simply because they were in the right place. It doesn't matter how great a hunter you are, if you're not where a big buck calls home, you'll never kill one. I've also had hunters hunt a day or two and just quit and move somewhere else.

I remember finding one 34-inch typical buck while scouting for a guy one year. The buck was incredible and the fact that he lived in an OTC unit made him an even rarer find. I put all the information on a map and sent it to the hunter. We even talked on the phone at length to make sure he knew how to hunt that buck. What happened? He called me on the second day and said he hadn't seen the buck and was going to try another place he knew of about 150 miles away! He never killed a buck – surprise! My point is, you have to get beyond the big picture if you want to hammer a smoker buck. The following is how I do my small picture research.

BOOTS ON THE GROUND

That's a tired old expression for getting out of your armchair and getting on the ground where the true action and fun really are. If at all possible, I try to visit my unit before I hunt it or even apply for it. There is simply no better way to find the bucks and their haunts than by showing up. While this can be called scouting, I think of scouting as actually "hunting" an area without a weapon before the season. Before I can do that effectively, I have to know where to look. There are up to four steps I take before I scout.

TALK TO THE LOCALS

Log on to any great forum and starting asking where to hunt big bucks and the hunters who really know what you're looking for just hide. You'll get information on great draw units and general information on OTC hunts, but not usually much that is specific enough to help in the small picture.

However, drive to some deer country and start talking to locals and you'll be surprised what you can find out. Because most good mule deer country is in rural areas, you meet some pretty nice folks out there. Since most locals are down-in-the-mouth about mule deer hunting (still stuck in the glory years), they'll often tell you every place big bucks have been killed, because they think it won't happen again. I've had that happen dozens of times and have followed up on the leads. More often than not, I find out something that helps me, even with tips that are a decade old.

If mule deer hunting is still pretty good in the area, then you can take advantage of the fact that the locals are proud of it and usually want to talk about it. If he is a hunter himself, he'll probably be evasive, so I don't pry. However, if you're lucky enough to meet someone who's not after big antlers, or is just a helpful person, you'd better listen carefully.

Just last fall I was scouting an area where I'd seen a tremendous buck the year before. He lived on a big hill with dozens of draws heading every direction. You could actually glass one of those draws from a public gravel road about a mile away better than you could from the hill itself. One morning just as the August sun was rising behind me, I was glassing intently from my pickup, hoping to catch the giant, when a man in his 80s pulled up on a Polaris Ranger. He asked what I was looking for and when I said mule deer, he shut off his machine and started talking.

Twenty minutes later I had a 50-year history on the mule deer hunting in the area. Although he didn't hunt anymore because the deer hunting had declined, he did tell me a place where a man who lived down the road had killed a 30-inch buck just the year before. I'd hunted the area before, and that information just confirmed that I needed to hunt it again! He also pointed to some country visible 10 miles away and said "those ridges always have bucks on them." While it might be a few years before I can visit the area he told me about, that's a hot tip I'd likely never have heard if I'd not talked to a local.

Just a couple years ago, I stopped at local convenience store in small-town Colorado. When the clerk learned I was hunting with a muzzleloader for bucks, he grabbed a napkin off the counter and drew a crude but accurate map to where he'd seen a few big bucks just a few weeks before. These leads don't always pan out, but I'd seen only one decent buck in five days of hunting, so I didn't have much to lose. I drove out to the area and started glassing. Within an hour, I'd found two shooters, and within several days had chances at two really big bucks. When in Rome, do as the locals do – or at least listen to them!

SHEEPHERDERS

Virtually every good mule deer book I've ever read mentions sheepherders as good sources of info (I think you could also add public-land cattle ranchers to the list), and my mule deer book will be no different. These stockmen spend months every year in some of the West's best big buck country. They are out early and late in the day when bucks are the most active and usually know where the best buck country is. Whenever I find these guys, I try to talk to them, which brings up a tip and a story.

I found this sheepherder in some extreme southeast Idaho backcountry talking on the phone! When he finally hung up, I asked him (in Spanish) if there were any big deer around. He flashed a gold-toothed smile and pointed across the canyon to some aspen stands. How's that for a hot tip?

While earning my bachelor's in English, I was required to declare a minor in a language or literature-related field. I've always been crazy and reconfirmed that to myself when I chose Spanish as a minor just so I could talk to the sheepherders. My dad had taught me as a youngster that the Basque sheepherders we'd frequently see in the summer knew where the big bucks lived. With that in mind, I enrolled in my first Spanish class when I was about 26. While I can barely find my way to the bathroom in Mexico, I can strike up a (basic) conversation with any sheepherder now. From these guys I've gotten dozens of great tips, two of which directly led me to killing my widest Idaho buck and my highest scoring Wyoming buck.

These guys are usually shy at first, but when they find out you can communicate with them, they usually become über-friendly. When one sheepherder by the name of Tomas Lozano found out I could speak some

Spanish, he insisted I camp with him one summer weekend when I'd been scouting some Idaho backcountry. He made me a dinner of freshly caught trout, rice, and garlic. When my horses broke loose and headed for the pickup, he quickly saddled his horse and handed it over to me to catch up with my errant mounts. One morning, he woke me at 4:30 and took me with him to check the sheep at first light. Along the way he showed me several basins and ridges where he'd seen big bucks. When I asked him about the best place in the area for deer, he pointed to a mountainside three miles away covered with broken spruce and aspen stands. "Mucho Venado allí," he said, which means many bucks over there. That just so happened to be the very mountainside where I killed my 36-inch-wide Idaho buck about seven years later. Take a Spanish class.

THE WARDEN

While these guys and gals can be hard to reach, they are truly the boots-on-the-ground personnel of state game departments. They spend ample time in deer country, talk to hundreds of hunters, and learn all kinds of things you need to know.

I remember back in the '90s there was an Idaho unit that I had heard held some good bucks, including a rumored 40-incher someone had recently killed. The unit was widely known for good elk hunting, but pretty much only the locals hunted there for deer. I tried several times to reach the game warden. I'd call the regional office and ask for her several times each week. They'd usually reply with a laugh and say, "She leaves before the office is open and sometimes we don't see her for two weeks." I'd left a few messages but hadn't heard back.

A month later, I accompanied a friend on an archery elk hunt in the same unit, hoping to gain some knowledge on the buck hunting there. We were packed in on horses about five miles up a drainage when wouldn't you know it, the game warden came riding into camp. As soon as I saw the braided ponytail sticking out from under a beat-up cowboy hat – and the narrow waist – I knew I'd found her.

After she checked our licenses, I mentioned that I'd tried to reach her earlier about mule deer hunting here. She remembered my calls immediately and apologized. She'd been working on a backcountry sting operation during that time, and had planned to call me once she was caught up at the office.

After about two minutes talking with her, I knew of several more good bucks that had been taken recently and what to expect from the unit. When I asked her where I should be looking for bucks, she spun around in her saddle and pointed to a big rough mountain a few miles away.

"I've checked a few hunters who've killed big bucks there recently. They still hunt around here, so they must think there's another one to shoot." She turned around and waved her hand toward the country behind our camp. "And that big rocky ridge above your camp is always good for a big buck."

Talk to the warden if you can.

AERIAL SCOUTING

Manned aerial scouting – done within the various state and federal laws governing its use – is an effective tool for locating buck country, and sometimes bucks. Most states now are on track to outlaw unmanned drones for scouting, and I concur. With no risk and low barrier to entry, soon the sky would be filled with drones.

Every time I talk about aerial scouting, someone gets his shorts in a knot and accuses me of breaking the law or being unethical. Personal ethics are just that – personal – so each person has to decide what is right for himself (some people think it's unethical to hunt with a rifle), but the law is the line in the sand that we can't cross.

Concerning the law, every Western state (and Boone and Crockett) has rules governing aerial scouting. These laws, among other things, govern the time and distance between flight and hunting. Most states require between 24 and 48 hours between flight and hunting and some, like Nevada, go further and restrict its use to outside of any open season (a good law by the way.)

I've spent a few hundred hours in the air over the decades flying buck country. I recommend nothing less than a Cessna 172 for flying in the mountains. I prefer a Husky, Super Cub, or Powered Parachute.

Aerial scouting is the best way to find buck country. Here's some Wyoming country that definitely warrants a look from the ground

Boone and Crockett bans trophies spotted from the air "followed by landing in its vicinity for the purpose of pursuit and shooting." A person in the air also cannot communicate to anyone on the ground in the vicinity or harass game from the air (that last one is a federal law).

My opinion is in line with these laws and rules, as I know if they are followed, aerial scouting does not give a hunter a decided advantage over his quarry. You still have to get on the ground and hunt that animal. Knowing where to hunt only helps the hunter focus his time and energy, just like using a trail camera or any optic for that matter. If you kill the animal, you still had to overcome the challenges of hunting within the law.

As a pilot myself, I've spent hundreds of hours in the air and flown a hundred more with other pilots. I only fly pre-season in the summer when scouting for

If you're lucky enough to catch bucks in the open, this is how they usually appear.

111

bucks that I might hunt. The closest I've ever hunted a buck I've spotted from the air is a week. Most cases it's a month or more. I use aerial scouting to narrow down the country to exact places to hunt.

If you plan on hunting a new area, I'd recommend finding an *experienced mountain pilot* who can show you the area. Don't just jump in a plane with anyone. Most pilots fly from airport to airport, which is completely different from flying close to terrain.

I use Google Earth to get a preliminary look at an area and narrow down where I want to fly, then share that information with the pilot. I also take a GPS and a notepad so I can note certain country to scout once I start ground scouting.

Make sure you understand all laws governing the country you want to fly. For example, some wilderness areas don't allow flights below 2,000 feet, while other areas have security issues – including flight restrictions over wildfire areas in the summer – that restrict aircraft. Always be respectful of people you may see in the area and keep your distance.

In 22 years of flying, I've spotted a half dozen really good bucks from the air, but have killed only one or two of them after the season opened. The value in aerial scouting lies in your ability to quickly learn a unit that is new to you.

This 200" Wyoming buck is one of the best I've spotted from the air. I took the photo in August and started hunting the mountain when the September rifle season opened. I never saw him again – as it often is with aerial scouting. However, I did find a honey hole that I plan to always scout when I get over that way.

SHED ANTLER HUNTING AND WINTER SCOUTING

I'm often asked about how shed antler hunting and winter scouting fit into my plans. I certainly think they are important, but not completely necessary. In most places, you will not be hunting bucks on winter range, so any information gathered there is really part of big picture research. I love to hunt

113

shed antlers, and it used to be a ritual for me. However, when I became a busy father and had to start focusing, I decided that shed antler hunting (done correctly) was just too much of a drain on my time and wallet, and wasn't all that important in finding bucks to hunt compared with all the other good information available to hunters. Also, with thousands of shed antler hunters out on winter range spooking deer, I could never convince myself I wasn't adding to the problem. In much of the West, mule deer survival is dependent on not being harassed on winter range.

I usually shed hunt now only if I've located a really big buck in the winter. At right is a picture of one of the few Boone and Crockett typicals I've seen over the years. I found him in early January and watched him until he dropped both antlers on January 17. While only about 26 or 27 inches wide, he had everything he needed to pass the 190" net minimum (assuming a 21" inside spread.) I later traded those antlers to my uncle/taxidermist for two full shoulder mounts, about $1,000 in value. If I could do that five more times, I might break even on all the money I spent shed hunting as a young man!

This is one of the few Boone and Crockett net typicals I've seen. After he dropped his antlers, I measured them at over 190" net, assuming a 21" inside spread.

Still, I do winter scout in some places. I typically just glass from long distances and let the wintering deer do their thing. In much of the West, bucks move miles between winter and summer, so all I'm really doing is enjoying the scenery and getting a feel for buck-to-doe ratios and genetic potential of the particular herd. In some places, I take a journal and count every deer I see. I've done this for years and my data usually tracks with the published data of the Game Department, so I know it's worth tracking.

PRE-SEASON SCOUTING

Once I know of specific places to look for bucks, the real fun begins. Nothing will motivate you to hunt hard like knowing where a big deer lives. According to my wife, I get a glazed-over look when I've scouted up a good buck and the season is about to open. I'll pack and repack my gear, shoot my weapon to the point I damage it (really, this has happened), and have a hard time accomplishing anything productive. Come deer season, I'm there for the long haul. I've hunted certain bucks 15 days straight (not really recommended), cashed in all my vacation time and begged for more, and pretty much worn myself razor-thin just because I knew where a big deer lived. If I can't scout an area, it's harder to hunt it hard, so I throw everything I have at the task.

By the time I'm ready to scout an area, I usually know right where I want to go. I'll make sure that I'm in the area both at first light and again just before dark, watching for bucks. I'll spend other hours of the day working out logistics on how to access the area, learning the trail system, and finding good places to camp. While the goal is mainly to lay eyes on the big one, I've also learned they don't always cooperate on my schedule. Sometimes just getting the logistics of how to hunt the area has to suffice.

If the area is a desert or water is just scarce, then of course I look for water sources. However, in much of the country I hunt, there's plenty of water so I don't get too focused on it. I'd guess a buck doesn't travel more than about a mile for water (I think it's less in most places), and I've found there's usually more water available, in the form of seeps, than we often think. If I do locate water in a dry area, I look for big tracks, which are the next best thing to seeing the buck.

I use 15x tripod-mounted binoculars a lot in the scouting season. Here are Vortex's 15x56 Vulture binoculars – good glass for the money.

I try to keep a camera handy when scouting.
Notice the swayback on this old buck.

A good buck I scouted one summer. I sneaked to within 60 yards and waited for him to stand. If only archery season would have been open!

I'll also place trail cameras on water sources if I think it's worth losing the camera over (always a possibility). Trail cameras have been a real game changer, and I've used them from desert areas to seven miles back into the high country. I think you need to use them, too, if you're close enough to deer country to check them often. I also find trail cameras are very effective on trails (who woulda guessed?) and are harder for a thief to locate.

I spent many days one summer scouting for a big non-typical I'd seen the previous year. The only glimpse I got all summer was a night shot from a trail cam I had set up on a trail.

You can double your chances by setting trail cameras on trails that go through saddles. I scouted one area four times from the ground and still never found the big deer I'd seen there the season before. I had cameras out and finally picked him up – at night – on a trail. Had I not had cameras out, I may have given up and moved on too soon.

Here I'm placing a trail camera on a trail far from water,
making it harder for thieves to find and steal.

If you live far from mule deer country and can't practically use trail cameras, don't worry. If I do a good job scouting, I can usually find out about the same information that a trail camera gives me, especially in country with plenty of water.

You can scout any time the season isn't open, but I find it most effective in late July and August. Depending on the area, some bucks don't even show up on their summer range until August. I found one area in Idaho that always held good bucks in July but by the time the archery season opened, they were gone. I learned later from a biologist who had intensively studied that herd that these bucks actually stayed in the low country until about August before moving into some higher elevation country (which was not high country) a few miles away. It always depended on the water year, too. In dryer years, the bucks moved up earlier while in wetter years they stayed low longer. That is why knowing your particular deer herd is so important; they all have different tendencies you can use to up your chances.

You have to be careful when scouting or you can actually decrease your chances. If you spook the bucks into the cover or out of the area, months of researching, planning, and scouting just went down the pot. I've learned this the hard way.

In 2011, after a very bad winter, I scouted all the areas I knew, hoping to turn up a good buck that had made it through the brutal conditions of the previous winter. I'd ridden horses, hiked, and even flew some of my honey holes, but could not find a buck over three years old. Finally in late August I spotted a big wide buck at timber's edge one morning at sunrise. I knew the mountain well and had a good idea of where he'd be by the October opener.

My mom loves to ride horseback in the mountains;
she's made more than a few of my backcountry scouting trips.

I showed up two days before the season and set up my camp. I was prepared to hunt a week and was just plain happy I'd found a big deer, considering there were so few available after the hard winter.

The day before the season, I got impatient and hiked around the mountain on a narrow horse trail toward the hillside I'd seen him on. I just wanted to get a peek at him and maybe know where to be at first light on the opener.

Hiking along at dawn, I noticed there were buck tracks in the trail from at least three or four bucks, and two of them looked like they were from big bucks. I had to choose between backtracking, climbing to the top and then glassing down, or continuing on the trail on the same level the bucks were on. I took the risky choice and stayed on the trail, convincing myself he probably wasn't in the group anyway as I still had a mile to go to get to where

I'd seen him. I should have studied the tracks more closely – I'd have realized they were only minutes old.

Not 200 yards down the trail, I jumped the herd (remember the season is still closed till next day). There were six bucks trotting away at 100 yards, spooked by my presence. I ripped the spotting scope out and got on them.

In the front was a buck about 30-32" wide with heavy bases – pushing six inches – and long beams to match his spread. His antlers were only about a foot or so tall and he had a huge body, indicating an old buck. Even without the height, he was a great buck few people would pass up – especially me. To make matters worse, there was a beautiful typical buck with the wide buck. He had "Booner" backs as I like to call really deep forks, and his left main beam was about 28" long and turned down near the tip. His gross score was over 190." Bucks like these are rare.

Scouting can be a pleasure. It's usually laid back enough that I can take my kids along on some trips. This is my daughter Sophia a few years back keeping an eye out for a big buck, Chapstick in hand.

I spooked them so badly that they hit the timber and turned downcanyon. I climbed 500 feet above their tracks and attempted to locate them in the canyon they'd headed into and then spent seven more days over two trips up there in search. Of course, I never saw those bucks again.

The mountain gets pressured quite a bit, and I would have had to get on him opening morning to have a chance, but if I'd just stopped and got above them when I saw the tracks, I probably could have had their home address opening morning. To find two bucks of that class in an OTC unit after a hard winter was a God-send – and I blew it. I still hang my head over that amateur move. Make sure when you scout, you do it as carefully as you'd hunt. Big bucks require a level of finesse few of us understand.

PART V: ESSENTIAL GEAR FOR THE BIG MULE DEER HUNTER

Besides your ability to find places big mule deer roam, to hunt smart and hard and be the bulldog of persistence, your gear will play an important role in your success. You can't trust your hard-earned hunts to gear that doesn't perform. As a rule of thumb, I buy the best gear I can afford. When I was younger, I often shopped at the army surplus store, used optics that weren't from the top of the heap, and drove old trucks (still do that, actually). However, I always bought and used good gear. I killed many of my big bucks using gear that wasn't part of any trend, but it always performed. As my financial outlook has improved over the years, so has my gear.

In the following section, I outline the essential gear every big mule deer hunter needs. I don't cover every single piece of gear, just the majors that can make or break a hunt. This gear has been refined and tested over three decades in all types of mule deer country.

WEAPON SYSTEMS

To kill big mule deer, I think you have to hunt with all three weapons types: rifles, muzzleloaders, and archery. Why? The answer is threefold. First, mule deer managers across the West have to figure out how to sell the most licenses with the least impact to the resource. Muzzleloader and archery seasons typically have lower success rates than rifle seasons. By offering these seasons, more people can hunt with less impact on mule deer.

The second reason a big mule deer hunter must consider all three weapon types is that draw odds have become so low across the West. If you're able to apply for only rifle seasons, your pool of good hunts just became much smaller.

Finally, by hunting archery and muzzleloader seasons, you can hunt mule deer at certain times of the year when they are more vulnerable. For example, the early archery seasons take advantage of the fact that big mule deer are still using the most open portions of their summer range and are easier to find. Some states, like Idaho, Utah, and New Mexico, offer early muzzleloader seasons. I've shot several good bucks, including a 190" typical, just in the last few years on early muzzleloader hunts. Other states offer hunts during the rut for muzzleloader and archery. One hunt just opened in southeast Idaho that allows archers to hunt some of the best big mule deer country in the West until late November. Rifle hunters lost that hunt about 1970, so by becoming a proficient archer, you can almost step back in time.

ACCURATE WEAPONS

Whatever weapon you choose, you must put accuracy at the top of the list when choosing your weapon. I don't buy into the mantra that precision accuracy isn't that important in hunting. Many hunters think a two-inch group at 100 yards is acceptable accuracy for a hunting rifle. "A mule deer's vital area is nine inches," they say. It is, but what they fail to consider is that two-inch group was shot under ideal conditions.

I've never killed a big mule deer under ideal conditions. Typically, I'm lying across a steep slope trying to dig my boots into the ground while keeping my pack from slipping as I steady my rifle on a buck that is about to spin and run into cover. Add in the fact that my adrenaline is peaking, the wind is blowing, and the buck just so happens to be the only big deer I've seen in a month, and I'll take the half-inch-at-100-yard rifle any day. It just lessens my chances of missing, especially as range increases.

Two years ago while muzzleloader hunting, I found an excellent typical buck grossing over 190" in a Colorado area thick with piñon pine and juniper. I could see the buck only by glassing across the canyon from two miles away. To kill him, I'd have to get in his living room. I noticed that he'd cross a powerline cut about 30 yards wide on his way to and from his bedding area each day. That was the only time he was really in the open. He never crossed in exactly the same place, but rather in area about 300 yards wide in the cut. He'd be visible less than a minute before reaching the cover on the other side. A clear shot would be near impossible unless I could catch him in the cut.

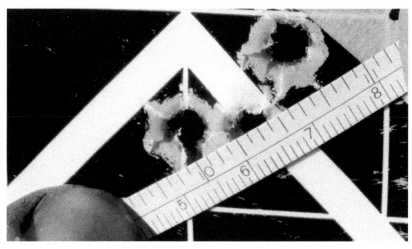

A three-shot 0.75″ group from my old Weatherby.
I demand an inch or less from my rifles.

My Cooper Excalibur
in 7mm Remington
magnum can deliver
three shots into a
half-inch group
at 100 yards.

I sneaked into the cut late one afternoon and sat down in the middle of that 300-yard area he'd been crossing. I was shooting a Khanke muzzleloader that year and had fired hundreds of rounds pre-season developing a load that would put two consecutive shots in a one-inch group at 100 yards with a peep sight (extreme accuracy for a muzzleloader). I was confident I could kill the buck if he showed up before dark, as the farthest I'd have to shoot was about 150 yards.

I sat about two hours as the sun sank low in the west. The huge trunk of a juniper tree broke up my silhouette. The shadows were slowly becoming long and the woods quieter. I'd seen or heard nothing other than a chipmunk that had scampered by a few feet away totally unaware of me. Tick tock, tick tock....

Suddenly I saw movement about 100 yards up the hill in the cover. I had to duck low to see under the low-hanging branches, but I was sure I'd seen the legs of several deer moving toward the cut. I raised my muzzleloader and checked the light coming through my peep. It was a little dark, so I unscrewed the adjustable aperture to let in more light. I was a little nervous and dropped the aperture. When I reached forward to pick it up, I caught more movement. Just stepping into the cut was a giant buck at 120 yards looking straight at me. He'd seen my movement. He was not the typical I'd seen before, but a much better non-typical. I quickly judged his spread at well over 30 inches and his gross score in the 220s. I got the gun up on my knee, but he had me pegged and took a step forward, which put him in a slight depression; only his backline and head were now visible. He was only one more step from the cover and it wasn't looking good for a clear shot.

Just then another buck stepped out into the cut. It was the typical I'd been expecting. He immediately read the body language of the bigger deer and turned and stared directly at me. A good buck in hand is better than a dozen in the bush, so I swung the gun right, held in the pocket behind his front leg and gently touched the trigger.

When the smoke cleared, I glimpsed the two bucks diving into the cover. It was getting dark, so I got right on their tracks. I found a few specks of blood. About 100 yards later, I noticed one set of tracks veered left. Studying the ground, I found a faint spot of blood with those tracks, so I quietly but quickly followed. Just a few minutes later, ahead in the broken cover, I could see the typical buck about 70 yards ahead checking his back trail. I had only a rump shot but knew he already had a bullet in him, so I held on the base of the tail and touched the trigger. He disappeared behind a cloud of smoke. I moved ahead and determined I'd hit him again. It was now almost dark, so I slowly backed out.

I was up at 4:00 a.m. after a short night of sleep and back on the mountain before first light. The full moon sank low in the western sky as I made the mile hike back into the area. As I picked up his track again, the sun hadn't yet risen. I tracked slowly and methodically with my gun ready at all times. It took an hour to pick his track from the litter of the forest floor. More deer had moved during the night, making his track harder to follow through the thick juniper jungle. About 150 yards into the tracking job, I found the buck piled up in three-foot-tall grass.

By the distance he'd covered and the length of his stride, I determined that he'd died within a minute or so of my last shot. Rolling him over, I could see my first shot had hit exactly where I'd aimed – in the pocket behind his front leg – but his angle when he looked at me was such that the bullet just

127

nicked his pericardium (the membrane around the heart) as it angled back and exited behind his paunch. The second bullet had hit within an inch of the base of his tail and had completed the job.

I killed this 191" gross typical Colorado buck by ambush with a muzzleloader. At 120 yards I had only seconds to make the shot count.

Had I been shooting the typical four-inches-at-100-yards muzzleloader common in the deer woods, I can't say for sure that I'd have killed this buck. I could tell you five more stories where the difference between punching my tag and entertaining friends with tag soup came down to accuracy. In the real world of big buck hunting where tension is high and mere seconds count, accuracy is king.

I'm currently shooting a Knight Mountaineer muzzleloader in 45 caliber. This gun consistently puts two shots under an inch at 100 yards with a peep sight.

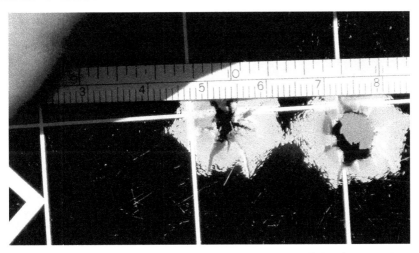

A 0.8-inch group from my Knight shooting Precision Rifle's Ultimate Conical.

Precision Rifles Ultimate Conical is a full lead bullet that
delivers accuracy and devastating wound channels.

BE A GOOD SHOT

You should have noticed that all of the hunters who influenced me were great shots – Grandpa, Dad, Cary Hansen, Kirt Darner – they wouldn't be great deer hunters if they weren't great shots. In the real world of buck hunting, shooting skill is everything.

Even if you buy the most accurate weapon possible, you still have to shoot thousands of rounds to become a good shot. I'm not a great shot – proficient yes, but not great. I'm not calm like those men I wrote about, so it takes more effort for me. I've worn out about three 7mm Remington Mags in my career. I shoot up to 2,000 arrows per year, and have fired thousands of rounds through muzzleloaders. I've got a long way to go, but I've also come a long way.

I don't agree that shooting off a benchrest isn't real-world hunting practice. Most of my shots in open mule deer country have been off a dead rest like a pack, a rock, or a tree, so shooting from a benchrest has plenty of application in the real world.

It's on the bench that you master your breathing, heart rate, and trigger squeeze. I do agree that you need to practice plenty off the bench, too, and I do. I absolutely love to shoot off-hand at rolling tires and water-filled jugs. In some cases, fastest man on the trigger gets the buck, and this type of practice makes handling your weapon second nature. Shooting is something you can involve your whole family in.

Being a good shot also comes down to knowing when to shoot and when to pass. Some of my misses were on shots that couldn't be made on "Impossible Shots," so I don't beat myself up too badly on those. Running shots beyond 100 yards, moving deer beyond 200 yards, off-hand, and Hail Mary shots should be avoided.

If you want to become fast with a rifle, practice on rolling tires; I practice at 25-150 yards. Quick handling of your rifle will become second nature.

I also practice shooting at water-filled jugs. Just have someone hide them in the brush then walk through and see if you can make the shot within three seconds of spotting the jug.

Mist is all you'll see when you make a direct hit.

Knowing when to shoot comes down to "hunting" bucks rather than either jump-shooting or pushing bucks – which almost always results in shooting at a moving animal and more misses and wounding loss.

If you employ the strategies I've written about in this book, you're likely to either get a close-range shot (my average range on big mule deer is less than 200 yards) or have a crack at an undisturbed buck that doesn't know he's in imminent danger. If you hunt right, your hits will skyrocket while your misses will plummet. If my memory is right, I've made about 90 percent of the shots I've taken at big mule deer over the last twenty years.

I'm currently shooting a Cooper Excalibur in 7mm Remington Magnum that can deliver three shots into a half-inch group, a Knight Mountaineer .45 caliber Muzzleloader that shoots one-inch groups with a peep at 100 yards, and an Athens bow that can keep my first shot in the kill zone out to 70 yards. Do what it takes to buy good weapons and achieve the most accuracy possible from them. You won't regret it.

My average archery shot on big mule deer has been over 50 yards. This Athens Convixtion can easily deliver killing arrows out to 70 yards.

In 2014 I switched from a fixed 3-pin sight to a 3-pin slider with 3rd axis adjustment. This Ascent bowsight is made by Montana Black Gold and has improved my accuracy in the typical steep terrain where big mule deer live.

HORSES

I've taken at least half my big bucks in the backcountry of Idaho, Wyoming, and Colorado where a horse was required to get in, get my buck, and then get him and my gear back out. I've also hunted hundreds of days in the backcountry in extreme weather conditions where hunting would have been near impossible if I didn't have horses to bring the proper camp gear.

Finding good bucks in OTC areas often means I have to cover a lot of country, and a horse is almost essential to do that effectively. I also hunt alone frequently, and having a horse to talk to is certainly better than nothing at all. You might chuckle at that one, but go spend nine days alone ten miles from the nearest road, and I'd bet you'll agree that a horse offers companionship that can keep your mood up, just like a dog does for most people.

I was lucky to grow up in a horse family. My grandpa was a sheepherder and rode horses hundreds of miles per year. He passed all that horse sense on to my dad, who taught me how to use horses in the backcountry. I've also been blessed to meet a few "real" cowboys who've deepened my knowledge of horses and packing.

Horse camp

I was lucky enough to meet a real cowboy, Bill Kelly of Boulder, Wyoming, while hunting the Hoback back in the early 1990s. Bill, an expert packer and a good friend, taught me a mountain of horse packer sense. Attesting to his true cowboy spirit, he later bought my daughter her first horse.

Bill Kelly bought my daughter her first horse.

If you have access to horses, I believe they can improve your success rate, especially if you're not in great shape and able to backpack, which brings up another point.

Fellow mule deer hunter David Long doesn't even own a horse, yet he is one of the top DIY mule deer hunters around. His primary method of pursuit is by backpack. I'd never argue against his method as it has proven very successful, especially in the early fall. I'm often asked if it's better to backpack for big bucks or use horses. "Both" is my answer.

A skilled backpack hunter has the advantage of being able to stay close to the bucks and keep a very quiet, inconspicuous camp, whereas a horse hunter can't really do that. If you know where the bucks are and you don't have to travel far for water, then backpack hunting is the way to go. Also, there are a few places where a backpack hunter can go but a horse cannot.

However, once the buck is down, this is where the men separate from the boys. Unless you just went in for the night, you're going to have 50 lbs. of gear and around 100 lbs. of buck to get back to the truck, so you're going to have two trips (really three if you count the original trip in) to be legal (many tickets are written to hunters who didn't bring out enough meat to qualify as a legal kill and avoid a "waste of game" citation). Many hunters completely underestimate this task. If it's only a few miles, most of us can handle that, but once you start getting two to five miles or more back in, only a few men can

137

handle the work required. For me, that is where a horse is imperative. In many places in the West, about the time you start thinking "How will I get a buck out of this place?" you're probably starting to get to the good hunting areas. A horse allows you to hunt without that limitation.

For me, I'll leave the horses home if logistically the area doesn't require a horse. Like if I'm hunting a pre-rut buck (rutting bucks can move miles a day) in an area three or fewer miles in, and where I don't need to travel more than about a mile from camp to hunt or more than 500 vertical feet to get water. Horses require much time and care during the hunt to keep them watered, fed, and rested, and if this time is better spent hunting a particular area, then I'll leave the horses home.

However, once I get into October where snow is almost a given in the high country, I rarely leave the horses home. I need a good camp with a woodburning stove to stay motivated enough to hunt effectively. Also, in some places and on some hunts, I need to hunt several areas that are miles apart to look at enough bucks to find a big one, so a horse is essential.

Horses have also added to the enjoyment of my hunting career to a degree that I cannot explain. There is just something right about hunting in the mountains from horseback. I do want to be clear that I've never killed a big buck while on a horse. Horses are too noisy to get close to big bucks in most country, so you have to be smart about how you use them or you'll just lower your chances at killing a big mule deer.

I could write a whole 'nother book on using horses for hunting, so just check my blog at rokslide.com and look for the category affectionately titled "Got Harses?" to learn all the techniques I use in packing horses. Before I move on to other essential gear, let's break for a horse story. This one took place in the backcountry of Wyoming in 2005.

HORSES, MOUNTAINS, AND MULE DEER

The blizzard packed 60 mph winds, almost drowning out the whinny of my saddlehorse tied in the spruce a hundred yards above. Working at a fevered pitch, I struggled to keep upright on the steep slope without stabbing myself. My packhorse, Missy, tied a few feet behind me, answered her compadre's call. With only one scraggly spruce to tie to at the kill site, I had to separate the horses, which were now my lifeline to get back to civilization.

The blood-stained snow was almost white again as the storm pounded the mountain. Trying not to fall, I cut along the spine to the hip joint, then twisted the last quarter until it pulled free. Loading it hastily onto my horse, I tied a basket hitch as best I could with my numb bare hands. The load was awkward, but the sawbuck was still centered on her withers. It should hold, I thought, as I make my way back up to the horse trail a thousand feet above. I slipped my still-bloody hands into some wet wool gloves. Tying the cape, head, and antlers onto the internal frame pack, I slung it over my shoulders. As much as I trust my horses, I don't want to roll one on a set of antlers that comes around only every few years.

The wind blew the snow horizontally, stinging my face, as I trudged back to my saddlehorse, Rain. In just the time it had taken me to quarter and load the buck, the storm had put down nearly six inches of snow on the six already there. Rain's whinny guided me in to where I'd tied her in the thick spruce. The storm ripped at the treetops above us like a hurricane. The slope leveled some there, so I sat on the ground next to the horses. I was totally exhausted.

I had planned to lead the horses to the top of the mountain to the trail, but there was no way I could buck the snow that far. I had killed the buck at noon after four hours of tracking him in the near-vertical terrain, just as the blizzard set in. I then had to retrieve the horses from the top, so I'd been bucking snow almost nonstop since first light. It was now 4:30 p.m. This was incredibly steep country to be riding horses in, but if I switchbacked enough, I should be able to ride all the way up. I decided to try to mount up.

Rain let me on, but the steepness of the slope caused her to struggle for her footing before I could get in the stirrups. She dropped her rear end and then came back up, hitting me hard enough to throw me. The deep snow broke my fall, but now the horses were loose. If I lost them, I'd never make camp and would have to stay out in this God-forsaken storm all night. I fought to my feet with the buck still on my back and lunged for the lead rope dragging behind Rain. I caught it by the last few inches and pulled hard to stop her. As badly as it had gone the first time, I had to try mounting again.

This time I cleared the saddle and got my foot in the stirrup before she started to struggle for her footing. She got her feet under her and I felt secure, so I tugged Missy's rope and spurred Rain. She kept her feet this time and started churning through the snow like a buzzsaw through timber. The cape and antlers got in time with her lunges, smoothing out the ride, and I held on tight.

We made good progress and hit the top within thirty minutes. I had dropped off the trail three hours before, and since then the high winds had crested the snow, forming a cornice that was four feet high. Rain leaned in and busted through the drift like a snowplow with enough force to throw me onto her neck, dislodging my feet from the stirrups. I would have fallen, but her next lunge threw me back into the cantle of the saddle and I was upright again. I was glad nobody was there to witness my flailing.

Finally we were on flat ground, but the unfettered wind was now blasting the full 60 mph to our backs, causing the mares to break into a trot. Normally I'd slow them, but I let Rain have her head as the sooner we got off the top and into the timber below, the better. The buck's antlers flopped wildly on my back, but a dozen or so half hitches still held them to the pack. Riding into the timber, the massive storm seemed to lose her grip on us and the horses slowed to a walk. I settled in for the long ride, thanking God I was off the top.

I rode an hour and a half around the mountain, slowly losing elevation as the black darkness set in. The snow had stopped, but the clouds held low to the ground. My headlamp penetrated the thick fog only a few feet, so I just shut it off and trusted the horses to stay on the faint high-country trail. Camp lay a few more miles ahead and the horses wanted to get back there as much as I did. Because of the storm, I was likely the only deer hunter in the miles of mountains that surrounded me, and I felt the emptiness of it all.

It was a welcome sound to hear my second packhorse, Charlie, let out a whinny in the pitch black as we neared camp. He had been tied in camp for over 12 hours and was just as happy to see us. I dumped my pack, pulled the panniers and the saddles, and made my way to my Eureka two-man tent. Because of the storm, the horses would have to wait until morning before I could graze them. Their long faces reminded me of their empty stomachs.

I leaned my rifle and the pack against the tent and lit a small gas lantern. The cold dark camp slowly came to life. I had tied a 6x8 tarp up next to the tent the day before as an extra shelter and amazingly, the wind had not taken it down. I noticed my poor Weatherby looked like an icicle. With the lantern at full power now, my eyes wandered to the cape and antlers. His antlers were some of the best I'd seen in fifteen years of hunting those Wyoming Mountains. I prayed and thanked God.

I really wanted to put a tape on him, but was too tired and cold. I dug through a pannier and retrieved some rice and soup. Warming it on my propane stove seemed to take forever as I sat shivering out in the weather. Occasional bursts of snow pellets blasted the tarp draped over my makeshift kitchen. The concoction was finally warm and I drank it straight from the pan, feeling the life-giving heat penetrate my body. I could relax a little now and I reflected back over the last few months. I'd hunted this buck for 16 out of the last 40 days, and it had ended as epically as a man could hope.

My pickup, parked at a lonely trailhead ten miles south, was still a four-hour ride down the canyon. I knew the storm would break during the night and tomorrow I could head back to civilization, fully satisfied with a hunt I will never forget.

It was 10:00 p.m. by the time I crawled into my military mummy bag. I still shivered from my damp long underwear, but knew in a few minutes that the bag would warm up and then so would I. As I drifted to sleep, I heard the faint sound of a horse pawing the ground a few feet away. The wind rushed over the ridge above, climbing to a howl before lulling a moment, then starting its climb again.

I thought back over the years of using horses in the backcountry and all the work it takes. Putting up hay in the hot July sun, the backbreaking job of keeping them shod, and the years of training it takes to get a horse ready for the mountains. I knew right then, it was worth it all.

Snowy camp in Wyoming.

NOTE: You may wonder why the page headers in this chapter are "Got Harses?" and I can say my editor made me do it. The phrase is from a blog post of mine a couple of years ago on the rokslide.com website. Here's an excerpt:

Nearly twenty years ago, while scouting fruitlessly for mountain goats in a remote Idaho unit, I ran into an old cowboy. Discouraged, I asked him where I might find the goats in that God-forsaken country. He moved his chaw into his left cheek, smiled and asked,

"Got Harses?"

I did and soon he was scratching a map in the dirt with a short stick. The next weekend, I made a 10-mile trip by horseback to the remote peak he said held goats. Just a minute after setting up the spotting scope, I could see furry white dots scattered amongst the cliffs. Had it not been for horses, I might have never found that country.

My grandfather was a sheepherder in the 1940s and relied on horses to make a living. He passed all that knowledge to my father, who made sure I had the chance to experience one of God's greatest gifts to mankind: the saddle horse.

You can read the full post at rokslide.com/easyblog/entry/got-harses

CLOTHING

PROBABLY SECOND ONLY TO MY WEAPON is my clothing's importance to killing big mule deer. If not properly clothed, humans get cold in temperatures much below 60 degrees. Some of the best mule deer hunting occurs in extreme temperatures (both cold and hot) and you must have the clothing necessary to hunt effectively.

My friend Mark Gillespie and I were caught in this Colorado high-country blizzard. In extreme weather like this, your clothing and your brain are all that stands between you and death.

For years, I used the affordable wool and polypropylene products widely available for my insulating layers. I'd also use a jacket with a breathable membrane for my outer layer to block wind and moisture. With high-end mountaineering style clothing now available to hunters though companies such as First Lite and Kryptek, and my finances improving, I've started using these products with success.

The clothing is lighter than the traditional products, and the comfort level is much better. Depending on the garment, performance is usually better, too. These companies also offer Merino wool base layers that are much more comfortable and retain far less odor than traditional wool. I've been using Merino from First Lite the last two years, and will never go back to the polypropylene underwear I used in the past. Merino might not be as durable (although all my garments still look fine with over 60 days of use) but it functions so much better in the scent control and wicking ability departments.

I'll still wear some cotton during hot weather hunts, but for the most part I'm wearing high-functioning synthetics and wools throughout the fall and early winter. Layering is still the best system, so I select my clothing based on that principle. Often I'm wearing the same base layer in December that I was in August, it's just that the December hunt requires many more layers.

Here's a rundown of my current layering system by First Lite.

Compression socks stay up in your boots, even pac boots, and are durable.

Merino wool, like that found in this Llano top by First Lite, outperforms traditional wool. I wear this top from summer scouting season through my winter weather hunts.

144

Allegheny bottoms. I wear these
from September into winter. If
the weather is warm, I switch
them out for the First Lite Merino
Red Desert Boxers
(not shown).

This First Lite Merino top called
the Chama is my next layer over
the Llano as temps stay below
freezing or I'm inactive.

On this recent November backcountry hunt, I wore First Lite's
Uncompahgre Puffy Jacket and Kanab Pant in Fusion camo.

If I'm riding horseback or glassing a lot in freezing temperatures, I add First Lite's North Branch pants (not shown) as an outer layer.

I mentioned earlier the great advancements in gear that sprang from the War on Terror. Kryptek Outdoor Group was founded by Butch Whiting and Josh Cleghorn, soldiers who served together in the Ninewa Providence in Northern Iraq. Butch and Josh discovered there that they had a common passion for big game hunting in extreme environments, and they channeled that passion into launching Kryptek when they completed their service to our country. Kryptek now specializes in ultra-high performance technical and outdoor apparel. As of press time, I have my first piece of Kryptek gear on order – a Dallibar II Jacket designed as part of a layering system. While I can't offer personal experience with Kryptek gear, many of the hardcore hunters on Rokslide swear by its performance, durability, and functionality. I'm sure I won't be disappointed.

I do need to emphasize that whatever clothing you select, it needs to be relatively quiet. A big mule deer's best defense is his hearing, and it's a rare hunter who realizes how often a buck detects him by the sounds he makes. If you don't worry about noisy clothing, you might as well not worry about whispering when you talk in the deer woods either.

If your budget doesn't allow for high-end clothing, then no worries. Notice in most of the photos in this book I'm wearing clothing that would be considered substandard by many of today's hunters. The bucks didn't seem to care what I was wearing when I pulled the trigger and at the time, those clothes were what I could afford and still have money left to chase bucks.

OPTICS PACKAGE

B ESIDES MY WEAPON AND MY WARM CLOTHING, my optics are my most important piece of gear – but knowing how to choose and use them is just as important as carrying them. I'll cover glassing technique later in the book; here I'll show you how I consider and choose optics. Over the last few decades, I've learned that I need three types of optics:

1) A binocular in 7x or 8x power (preferably range-finder equipped)
2) A spotting scope with 25-60 power (fixed or variable)
3) A 15x-20x binocular (tripod mounted)

Left to Right, Vortex Vulture 15x56,
Swarovski CTC 30x75, Swarovski EL Range 8x42.

BINOCULARS

Because mule deer hunting is typically an active pursuit, I've found that the lower powers of 7x or 8x serve me best. A steadier viewing image trumps more magnification in my book, and the lower power binoculars deliver that

149

steadiness. I also prefer the wider field-of-view of a lower power to catch bucks in the peripheral view. Finally, low power binoculars are brighter than their higher power counterparts when all other variables are considered equally. A higher power binocular must have a proportionally bigger objective lens to match the brightness of the lower powers, which adds weight and bulk.

I've tried a multitude of 10x to 12x glass and hunted with many hunters who use them. Once in a while, someone who's carrying the higher powers will spot a buck I've missed, but more often I'm showing him bucks that he didn't pick up with the bigger glass. If I'm actually looking at a buck, and have time to mount them on a tripod or rest them against a stationary object, then yes, the higher powers are better. However, hunting isn't just looking *at* bucks, but *for* bucks.

Often I'm still-hunting along and need to check something in the distance. I usually can't sit and steady myself and still see above the vegetation, nor is there a tree or rock handy to lean against. I have to be able to widen my stance, pull my elbows to my chest and tighten the optic to my face to get steady. I do this dozens to hundreds of times in a typical hunting day and this is why for me the lower power binoculars are better. With the wider field of view a lower power binocular offers, I'm also more likely to pick up bucks in the peripheral area of the image.

I mount my binoculars on a tripod even if I'm on a vantage point. While a higher power has an edge, I still find the lower power works in an excellent fashion from a tripod. It's like studying a photograph shot in high definition. I've found hundreds of hidden bucks doing this. Most lower power binoculars don't have a 1/4-20 insert for a tripod mount, so I just set the binoculars on the flat top of my Manfrotto 342RC2 tripod head, sling the strap around my neck (in case I knock them off) and glass away. This saves me time, gadgets, and weight in my pack.

Using a quality low-power binocular on a tripod is like watching a movie in HD. I've glassed hundreds of bucks this way.

You must also learn to properly focus your binoculars to each eye. Some hunters glass a lot but still don't know how to properly focus their binoculars. Virtually everyone has a dominant eye and your binoculars must be set first to each eye before your center focus wheel will work at maximum performance. I always set the initial focus of my binoculars *while they're mounted on a tripod* and fixed on an object with high contrast (like a white-barked aspen against a dark background) between 300 and 500 yards. Trying to hand-hold and set the focus will produce subpar results. Depending on the binocular, you usually focus the right eye first on that eyepiece (with your left eye closed) then vice versa for the left eye, adjusting with the center wheel. Once the optics are set, lock down or note your settings. With your focus set to each eye, now you need to change focus only on the center adjustment, which in the majority of brands adjusts the focus for both eyes simultaneously.

I've been carrying a rangefinder for about a dozen years now. If you're hunting with archery or muzzleloader equipment or plan to shoot a rifle beyond 200 yards, do yourself and your quarry a favor and carry a rangefinder. Some argue it's just one more unfair advantage over the animal. So are Gore-Tex boots if you really want to argue advantages, so I say get a rangefinder and improve your ability to kill humanely. If you use it right,

you'll also know when you need to get closer to make a better shot – the best way to improve your hit-to-miss ratio is to know when to shoot and when to hold your fire.

The problem with a rangefinder is that it is just one more gadget hanging around your neck. When rifle hunting, my rangefinder invariably ends up in my pack once I grow tired of having it in the way. When archery or muzzleloader hunting, I keep it around my neck, but it always seems an inconvenience and makes extra noise. Big bucks don't put up with much noise or movement, even at hundreds of yards away. Juggling both a binocular and a rangefinder just ups the odds of their detecting me. The solution is to carry a combination binocular/rangefinder.

I used a Swarovski Spotting scope for years with great success and really believed in Swarovski's optical performance. In 2014 I started using Swarovski's EL Range 8x42 binoculars. This top-tier binocular/rangefinder combo solves the problem of fiddling with two instruments.

I've put a full season on them now, and the ultra-clear and bright viewing experience and ruggedness line up with everything else I've come to expect from Swarovski – and I no longer have to carry both a rangefinder and binocular. The battery life is also exceptional; I never changed the battery in the five months between scouting season and hunting season. The rangefinder works between 32 and 2,000 yards, and rarely do I have to hit the button more than once to get a reading. There is also a built-in inclinometer that calculates the "shoot-to" distance in steep terrain. I've missed big mule deer shooting at steep angles because a bullet doesn't behave like it does when shooting shallow angles. If the angle is enough to change your point of impact, the EL Range calculates it. I've tested it up to 50-degree inclines with superb results. I'm taken back at the edge this one feature gives a hunter in the varied terrain of the West.

The view through the Swarovski EL 8x42 with the inclinometer turned on. The top number is the actual distance to the tree; the bottom number is the distance you aim for. This technology has improved accuracy beyond belief.

If there is a chink in the armor of the ELs, it is the lower range limit of 32 yards. As a bowhunter, I sometimes need to read distances shorter than that, like when trying to sneak an arrow below a branch at a bedded buck on a steep slope. Talking with other owners of the ELs, they say if it's shorter than 32 yards, you don't need a rangefinder. I'd almost agree, but would crown the ELs perfect in all categories if they ranged down to 20 yards. The price is steep but if you consider you're buying high-end binoculars and a high-end rangefinder simultaneously, the price is easier to swallow. If you can't swing the price tag of the Swarovski, there are other less expensive brands out there; I can't vouch for them as I haven't used them.

There's always a debate on how much a hunter should spend on glass. The old axiom "buy the best you can afford" is the best guideline. You may have noticed from the older photos that early in my career I used Pentax binoculars. They are certainly not considered high end binoculars but I killed many a good buck while using them, including two of my best. As I was able to make more money, I bought better binoculars, but my success didn't jump substantially. It's the hours *behind* the binoculars that makes the biggest difference, so get that right first before you max out a credit card hoping Brand X is finally going to get you the big mule deer.

If you want to read a pile of reviews on good glass from mid to high range, check out Rokslide.com and look for the Optics Reviews. We've had a hard-core optics following since Rokslide's inception and consequently have many good reviews on glass.

SPOTTING SCOPE

A good spotting scope, or spotter as they're often called, is essential in most deer country in the West. Don't falsely assume a spotter is just for studying antlers. Spotters should be used to spot bucks that are either out of reach of binoculars or are obscured by shadows and vegetation. I estimate that I carry a spotting scope 80 percent of the time I'm hunting. The only time I don't is if I'm still-hunting or ambush hunting in thick cover. I think a spotting scope is underutilized by many hunters; a good spotter allows you to spot bucks at up to five miles away if the conditions are right. When you start covering that much country, you're far more likely to find a big mule deer.

I'm currently using spotters from Swarovski, after purchasing my first one in 2003. I've tried Leupold, Zeiss, Bushnell, Bausch & Lomb, Vortex and others, but I think Swarovski is the top spotter out there if you can afford one. If you can't, I'd lean toward Vortex spotters. Through my association with Rokslide and my field trials, I can tell you you get a lot of scope for the money and world-class customer service with Vortex.

WHAT POWER?

I'm often asked what power spotter is best. I think you'll spot most bucks around 30x as that is where clarity, brightness, and steadiness seem to be the best. Less than 30x and you're leaving some magnification on the table, but if you're much above 30x, you'll start to see vibrations (in real hunting conditions, wind is the norm), mirage, less field-of-view (I spot a lot of bucks in the peripheral view of my optics). You also lose light because the ratio of the objective lens to the ocular lens decreases as magnification increases. A 60x spotter is nice but you'll find that you spend very little time at 60x in real hunting conditions. In order for 60x to work in low light, you'll need a huge objective lens, ideally in the 80-90 mm range, which means more weight.

BEST SPOTTER FOR THE BACKCOUNTRY HUNTER

If you're on a budget like I am, you probably look in wonder at the high-end HD spotting scopes out there and just dream. These scopes are incredible tools for the mule deer hunter, but you could buy a pretty good used pickup or a great Mexican vacation for the price. I've always believed you should buy the best optics you can afford, but I must admit that there are optics that I can't afford! However, I found about a dozen years ago that you can experience near-HD quality at less than half the price.

Swarovski makes the CT extendable spotting scope. It looks like the telescopes the old sea captains used, in which the sections of the barrel slide inside each other when collapsed. In the CT, this allows for a roof prism design and a lighter, more compact spotting scope than the traditional porro prism designs. While not well known in North America, the CT design is popular in Europe.

There are two CT scopes available: The CTC 30x75 (comes with fixed-power eyepiece) and the CTS 85 (requires that you buy an eyepiece). I own the CTC 30x75. I know our local dealer personally and before my purchase, he let me take a gently used CTC 30x75 spotting scope outside of the shop for a day along with a used Swarovski 20-60x 65mm spotting scope. I scouted some winter range east of town for a few hours with these scopes.

Side by side, the CTC 30x75 was clearer and brighter at the same power than the 20-60x 65mm scope. The 75mm objective lens also had a noticeably wider field of view. The CTC is also 10 ounces lighter and four inches shorter.

As with most things in life, there are trade-offs. Obviously, with a fixed 30-power, I can't zoom in like a variable scope can, but I find anything above 40x power difficult to get steady in real hunting conditions, so I'm really giving up only about 10 power.

The dealer told me that because of the collapsing nature of the CT design, they are not sold as waterproof. This concerned me, so I called Swarovski directly. They said while the CT scopes are not waterproof, one of their biggest U.S. markets for the line is Alaskan guides. It doesn't get much wetter than Alaska, so I forked over the $500 for the used scope.

At 44 ounces, the Swarovski CTC 30x75 may just be the ultimate backcountry spotting scope.

I've now had my CTC 30x75 for over a dozen years, spending hundreds of hours looking through it. I can attest that it is a great scope for the money. It has ridden hundreds of miles in a saddlebag and a backpack and has been used well over those miles. It has great edge-to-edge clarity and is usable almost to the end of legal shooting light at reasonable distances.

I had minor fogging problems twice in the first few years (I hunt the nasty snowstorms on purpose, so my optics get wet a lot). Both times, I was able to defog the scope in less than five minutes by warming it with body heat or direct sunlight. Because I learned to wipe the inner tube off with a handkerchief before sliding the scope together, I've never fogged the scope since then.

If you are interested in the CTC 30x75, shop ahead. They are a special-order item so your dealer will need some time to get one. Checking the internet, I found several dealers who could get them and found two scopes for less than $1,100 new. I also found a used one for around $600. As Swarovski has a lifetime warranty, I wouldn't be afraid to purchase a used one again. I did strip out my mounting threads once (my fault for not getting the scope down tight) and sure enough, Swarovski fixed it for free once I paid the postage.

Swarovski ATS 25-50 x 80mm

Last summer, I struck a deal between Swarovski and Rokslide to test a few loaner spotting scopes. I could try whatever I wanted, so based on what I've written here, I ordered their ATS 25-50x 80mm in an angled design. I put about 30 days on the spotter last fall. I really liked it and the optical performance matched the 30x CTC, plus I had the benefit of going to 50x if needed. The extra performance, though, comes with a weight and size penalty. If I keep the scope for the 2015 season, my plan is to use it on all my scouting trips (I don't need as much gear for scouting so weight isn't as critical) and hunting from road camps, but I'll use my old 30x CTC for my backcountry hunts where weight and size matter.

One other benefit to the 25-50x was its digiscoping option. Using an Olympus OM-D E-M5 that Aron Snyder *gave* me, I was able to take photos of bucks out to 1,200 yards with stunning clarity and full field of view. This is the first digiscoping option that produced results nearly as good as the big 500mm high-end camera lens I've used over the years. Most digiscoped photos are of poor quality, but not these.

The Swarovski ATS 25-50 x 80mm is a pleasure to glass through.
At 59 ounces, it is a great scope for all hunts where weight isn't critical.

I took this photo from nearly 1,000 yards using the Swarovski ATS
paired with an Olympus OM-D E-M5. I'm stunned at
the optical performance of this digiscoping system.

HIGH POWER TRIPOD BINOCULARS

In the early season, before the freezing temps and snow hit, I glass more. This is for several reasons:

1) The big bucks are typically in the open country and are easier to spot.

2) Warmer temps means I can sit longer without moving.

During this time, I find a high-power (15-20x) tripod-mounted binocular very valuable. I started messing around with high-power binoculars over 20 years ago. My dad had an off-brand set, and though they were barely tolerable, I discovered the advantages of glassing with both eyes open. Not coincidentally, I killed my widest buck to date after spotting him from three miles away one early October day with a pair of 16x50 tripod-mounted binoculars. With a good pair, I can comfortably take apart the country from short-rifle range to five miles. Being able to glass without eyestrain will lead to longer glassing sessions and more bucks spotted. While high-quality spotting scopes like my Swarovski CTC 75 are excellent optics, by design you're forced to glass through one eye, which is not the way God wired your brain – you'll spot more bucks with both eyes open. If I'm limited by weight or space, I'll take only the spotting scope, but if I can bring both, it's like having and eating my favorite cake (Jodi's cherry-chocolate cake, for the record).

Last year I arranged a trade with Vortex to try their new Vulture HD 15x56 binoculars. At under $500, these are designed for the hunter who just can't spend $1,000 or more for Vortex's highly rated Kaibab 15x56 binocular.

Vortex's 15x56 Vulture tripod binoculars proved to be a good value.

I put a few dozen hours on the Vultures through the scouting and hunting season and they served me well. I found their clarity good and their brightness exceptional, both provided with no eyestrain. They were a little finicky on focus adjustment (very fine adjustments) but once I figured that out, they were great. I have not tried the Kaibabs so I can't compare the two but I'm sure it follows the axiom "buy the best you can afford."

FOOTWEAR

LIKE CLOTHING, FOOTWEAR HAS THE POTENTIAL to make or break a hunt. You need to really pay attention to your feet and spend ample pre-season time preparing for the rigors of the hunt. You can't hunt on lame feet, and thousands of hunts are cut short each year because of footwear problems.

I don't have very finicky feet and other than a very wide forefoot (4E), I can find a variety of footwear options that perform well for me. Some hunters aren't so lucky and need professional help in selecting proper footwear.

I recommend buying only footwear that you can return within a reasonable time. That means you have to purchase well before your hunt and figure out, wearing the footwear indoors (required by most manufacturers if you want a return option), whether it will perform on the hunt.

The Tek-Light Hunter by Lathrop & Sons is a good early season boot for rough rocky terrain. Allow a break-in period, as they are one tough boot.

I recommend buying from a professional bootfitter such as Lathrop & Sons, who have decades of experience in podiatry (the science of the feet), or from high-end boot stores such as Schnee's of Bozeman, Montana. You can't skimp on footwear and these pros can seriously improve your footwear experience. You'll pay more money when you do it right, but if you pay twice as much for a top-end boot that fits perfectly, and it lasts twice as long (very likely) as the shoddy options at Wal-Mart, the math shows you'll break even *but* have a much better experience. That's worth it to me.

I typically wear a light hiker in the August/September months. The weather's better then and I'm typically hunting with archery or muzzleloading gear and need to stalk in close, so quiet stealthy footwear is a must. I'm currently using the Bridger made by Schnee's. It is a light boot great for stalking in the early season.

Once I get into October and the rifle hunts, I'll wear a heavier boot with light insulation. The breathable materials available today are great at keeping moisture out, but also keep some moisture in regardless of manufacturer claims, and on extended hunts with no heat in your tent, they can become cold and damp because they never fully dry. I can manage this until the snow flies, but then I switch to a pac boot with removable liners.

I'm currently using the Hunter II from Schnee's Boots. A removable liner means you can easily dry your boots and leads to warmer feet the next day. I also use the chemical boot heaters shaped like a sole on hunts where the temperature never gets above freezing. For a few bucks and a few ounces per day, these can really make a difference.

Hunter II from Schnee's Boots

DEER CAMP

I F YOU'RE STAYING OUT EVEN ONE NIGHT in the woods, deer camp is as important as your clothing. I learned from my sweet daddy many years ago that camp has to be comfortable and even a little fun if a mule deer hunter is going to succeed. A good camp not only allows you to thrive in inclement weather, it also allows you to stay for the duration while you search for the buck of your dreams. It's in camp that you recharge yourself in preparation for another day of hunting. If your camp isn't comfortable enough to recoup physically and mentally, by about day two you'll be thinking about mamma and your warm bed at home. Before you know it, you'll have dreamed up all kinds of excuses to leave – the bucks are gone, work's calling, too much hunting pressure, I saw a scary snake, whatever – and it's only a matter of time before you're at the truck. Generally speaking, I have two types of camps: a road camp and a backcountry camp.

ROAD CAMP

I've killed several of my best bucks from road camps. These are great in areas where you can reach good buck country in less than an hour and in areas where you need to cover a lot of country to see enough bucks to find a dandy. Road camps can also serve as a base camp to a spike camp in the backcountry. I've hunted up to two weeks straight in the backcountry and sometimes need to return to the truck to resupply. If that might be the case, I make sure I at least have a tent set up or a cot in the horse trailer so if I get caught in the dark or just need a break, I'm not forced to sleep in the pickup – which really doesn't give you much rest at all.

Staying in a road camp allows you to be more mobile
and enjoy a few of the niceties of home

My road camps will have many of the niceties of home, like a good comfortable cot with a thick mattress and full-sized pillow. I'll bring propane stoves, lanterns and space heaters and, of course, good groceries. I also set up a wall tent if I'm hunting with other guys, or if I'm alone, I'll set up a six-man or eight-man tent. Big buck hunting is more mental than physical, and these comforts allow me to stay sharp enough to hunt to the often-bitter end. Just last fall, I killed a 180-inch gross mule deer on the very last morning of a 10-day hunt. My success, in part, came from the fact that I could recharge nearly every day in my road camp, and with access to a vehicle, I could cover a bunch of buck country to find what I was looking for.

BACKCOUNTRY CAMP

Just because I'm hunting miles away from a road for days on end doesn't mean I need to put up with a shoddy camp. I've learned this the hard way, and have seen many other hunters who've left the mountain just as the hunting was getting good because of a subpar camp. I'll give you a breakdown of the major pieces of gear I take into the backcountry.

TENT AND WOODBURNING STOVE

I always take a tent a little bigger than I need. In the early fall before the big snow hits, a woodburning stove is not needed, so I'll take a backpacking tent a man-size bigger than what I need, so a two-man tent if I'm solo or a three-man if I'm with a partner. I need to be able to put everything in the tent if the weather turns, so having that extra space is necessary. It makes no sense to pack a one-man tent and then bring a tarp for cooking or for covering gear.

Last year, my friends at 1-Shot Gear in Denver loaned me a Hilleberg Nallo 3GT. This three-man tent was awesome in both construction and livable space. I could cook in the vestibule and still have plenty of room to get in and out of the tent. I also own an old two-man Eureka that has served me well for 10 years, proving that you don't always have to break the bank to get decent gear.

The Hilleberg Nallo 3GT provides ample living space
for two backcountry hunters and their gear.

Once I get into October and subfreezing temperatures and deep snow are possible, I bring a tipi-style tent in the six-to-eight-man range. That sounds huge, but if you're hunting 5-10 days and the weather goes sour, you'll use all that space, especially with a partner. Again, camp should be the place I can recover mentally, and if I'm unable to stand up in the tent or I'm constantly tripping over my gear, I start to get a little grumpy.

I used Army Surplus 8-man insulated canvas tents for nearly 20 years. They can still be had for around $200 and are warmer than any modern tent design you'll find out there. They also are great at preventing condensation. They are heavy – around 30 pounds – and are suitable only for road or horse camps.

I've spent over 400 nights in these tents.
For the money, they can hardly be beat.

Last fall, I finally switched to a modern lightweight tipi, this one an 8-man from Seek Outside of Ridgeway, Colorado. I stayed more than 20 nights in mine, from 15 degrees and snowing to 80 and sunny. It performed well, although next year I'll add a liner to prevent condensation (always a problem with the waterproof fabrics) and improve the insulation factor. Kifaru International also makes some excellent ultralight tipi tents.

This brings up the necessity of a woodburning stove. There is something comforting about fire beyond the heat it provides that I believe was placed in the heart of man by God Himself. Ancient hunters on every continent scratched pictographs of fire alongside their hunting scenes. Many hunters think of fire as a survival tool, but it's way more than that. If the weather's cold and you stick me in a tent with no heat source, I'm good for about two days. Throw in a good woodburner and big bucks watch out! I'm there for the duration. A good woodburner can cook your food and dry your clothes and boots – and warm your heart and your attitude.

Seek Outside's Ultralight 8-Man Tipi

Lightweight Titanium woodburning stoves like those made by Kifaru and Seek Outside make it easier than ever to hunt in extreme backcountry weather. Shown: Seek Outside's Titanium XL woodburner

I used to pack heavy iron stoves pre-season into the backcountry for later use, but that is almost unnecessary these days with the invention of the lightweight Titanium Stoves by Kifaru and Seek Outside. Even backpack hunters can now carry a functioning woodburner for not much more weight than their cooking stove (which of course they won't really need with a woodburner in camp).

LET THERE BE LIGHT

I'd rank a good light source as a close second to a woodburner for providing comfort in the backcountry. I've lived with nothing but a small maglight for days on end, but if I bring a good lantern, it just improves the camp mood. Like fire, light brings an unexplainable comfort to the hunter. I still prefer white gas lanterns, as they perform well in subzero temperatures and I'm not stuck with the dilemma of what to do with an empty fuel canister at hunt's end – I pack fuel in burnable water bottles. If I take a cooking stove, it's white gas, too, so no need for two fuel types. If it's summer scouting or September, I'll just use a good headlamp as the nights are pretty short.

SLEEP SYSTEMS

If I'm spending more than a few nights in the backcountry and I'm horsepacking, I bring a cot. Cots provide more comfort than sleeping on the ground and create a storage area underneath that can help keep your tent space more usable. If I can't bring a cot, I spend extra time leveling the ground where I'll sleep, and bring a great sleeping pad. As a horsepacker, I often double-blanket my horses. The top blanket doesn't touch the horse, so it stays clean and odor-free. In camp I use the top blankets as extra sleeping pads. Again, a good camp allows you to rest, and if you can't get comfortable while sleeping, your motivation to hunt will wane.

I use down sleeping bags for their great warmth-to-weight ratios. Down can lose its insulation factor if it gets wet, so you have to be very careful. I cover mine with a light plastic tarp and have never had much of a problem. Your tent is the most important factor in keeping your bag dry, so if you're using a shoddy tent, down is probably not a good choice. I find that no matter the tent, if I just take the time to dig a drainage system around my tent, I can prevent water from entering even in the worst downpours. Some guys can sleep without a pillow, but not me. In my horse camps, I bring a good pillow, but in my backpacking camps, my puffy jacket has to do. No matter your choices, make sure your sleep system allows you to get the needed rest hunting requires.

MISCELLANEOUS

For my horse camps, I line one of my panniers with a lightweight 3/16" piece of paneling that can serve as a table in camp. I bring four wood screws and then attach "legs" I make from tree branches. I also bring a lightweight folding chair like the Helinox sold by Mystery Ranch of Bozeman, Montana. A chair is key to relaxing and recuperating in camp if you're there for more than a few days. If I can choose only a chair or a cot, I'll take just a cot; it will work in place of a chair. If I'm in a backpacking camp, I'll make a sheepherders chair, which is two logs about 12" in diameter placed close parallel and secured together with wood stakes or rocks so they don't roll. You can sit in the crotch between the two logs.

I bring a 12" square of aluminum foil; it has numerous uses for cooking. A Leatherman with pliers, knives, and a small saw (great for cutting trekking poles) is always on my belt and I use it daily. Last year, I added a Havalon Piranta to my camp gear and found it superior to traditional knives for breaking down and caping a big buck, except around the eyes and cheeks where it's easy to cut through the thin skin. In my horse camps, I bring a collapsible water bucket so I can have plenty of water within reach. If I'm running a woodburner, I either bring a small pulley to secure in the apex of the tent so I can hoist my upside-down boots every night (air temp can reach 100 degrees up there), or I pound long thin stakes in the ground so I can put my boots above the stove where heat collects. I bring a handful of clothespins, handy for drying clothes, and I always bring a SPOT locator – and usually keep it in my shirt pocket so I don't get separated from it. If I have to choose between a phone and SPOT, it's the SPOT every time. In that same shirt pocket are also two firestarters: Trioxane tablets and a cotton/paraffin tablet – and two lighters that I replace every year – and I don't use them for anything else in camp.

While every hunter's gear list will vary, everything that I mentioned here is on mine every year. I've included my main gear list in the back of the book.

PART VI: TECHNIQUES TO KILL THE BEST BUCK OF YOUR LIFE

Well, we've finally arrived. I've spent a good chunk of this book giving you a history of mule deer, defining exactly what a big mule deer is, and preparing you mentally and physically for the hunt. We dove into how to research and find good areas, becoming a good shot, and selecting the essential equipment. I wrote all that in preparation for what's to come, both in this book and what lies ahead when you finally head out for mule deer country. Now all you need are the techniques to kill the best buck of your life.

In this section, I give you all I've got ... everything that has proven essential to me in killing all the big mule deer I have. This is where we leave luck at the truck and take our skills to the mountain. Many hunters say "I'd rather be lucky than good," but I say "I'd rather be good than lucky." Luck is finicky but your skills are dependable. It is our skills that we can depend on and it is our skills that we must continually practice and refine.

Now I'll lay out the nine hunting techniques you must master if you want to kill a buck that scores more than 170."

Twenty years ago, if I killed a big deer, I thought my success resulted from hunting the right area. Now though, if I get a big buck on the ground, I know the right area is only second (and a far second) to how I hunted the deer. While showing up might be half the game in many pursuits, it's just not so in big buck hunting. I know many hunters who've spent years in good deer country but have yet to kill a big deer. They are obviously in the right place, so what's the holdup? They don't hunt the area correctly, that's what the problem is. They are too focused on the "where" instead of the "how."

I've drawn only two really good tags in my lifetime: a Colorado tag in 2010 where I killed a 200" buck, and a Utah limited-entry tag in 1997 where I got skunked, even after scouting for eight days pre-season and hunting hard the entire 11-day season. On both hunts, there were more than a few five- to ten-year-old bucks available, and hunting pressure wasn't bad. So why did I kill a 200" buck on one and come home empty-handed on the other? Hunting technique is why.

I was only 28 when I drew that Utah tag. While I did a pretty good job on it, and even had a quick chance to shoot a 30" non-typical, I didn't hunt the unit right. First, although I scouted for eight days, that still wasn't enough. Good unit or not, you need more like 20 days to get a real feel for the unit, and that is why I don't like draw hunts; you can't learn them thoroughly like units you can hunt yearly.

Second, I covered way too much ground once the season opened; I'd walk five to eight miles per day. While that sounds pretty "he-man" and seems a badge of honor nowadays, I've learned since then that big bucks live within about a square mile and you need to be there and nowhere else. Slowing down and hunting right is the key.

By the time I drew Colorado, I was 41 and had another 13 years of tuition paid to the school of hard knocks (your best teacher). I knew by then that it does me no good to run to and fro during the season. Focus on areas that are known buck hideouts – thick, nasty, hard to access – and be in them daily. I rarely walked more than a few miles a day on that hunt, ensuring I wasn't polluting the country that I hunted. The 200" buck I found at last light the third day had actually seen me, but I was moving slowly enough that he didn't peg me as immediate danger. This gave me the critical seconds needed to make a killing shot. You can watch the video of that hunt on my blog at Rokslide.com by searching "Why We Do What We Do."

A buck that is five years or older possesses senses and instincts that are far and above ours and those of the other deer in the herd. To kill one on purpose, you have to hunt in a way that you don't spook them until it's too late for them to get away. It's your hunting techniques that will get you the shot – from recognizing buck country, to learning how to move in deer country, obeying the wind, still-hunting, ambush hunting, tracking, deer drives, long-range hunting, and finally glassing – and I'll cover all nine techniques.

HUNTING THE COVER, THE LAST FRONTIER

Before we dive into the nine techniques, I need to frame the picture I'm about to paint to make sure you understand how and where to apply the techniques. The techniques will work anywhere mule deer are found, but if you want to at least double your success rate, you need to lose any aversion to hunting in and around *cover*. By cover I mean anywhere deer spend the daylight hours. It could be an oakbrush jungle in Colorado, a stand of Idaho maples, a piñon/juniper forest in southern Utah, or a manzanita tangle in California – any thick vegetation where mule deer seek security. I've killed about half of all my big deer at between 40 and 120 yards in and around cover. I've killed only two at over 400 yards. Had I not hunted the cover, my success rate would be half what it is.

I wrote an article for the magazine *Hunting Illustrated* about hunting in the cover for big mule deer. Like most articles that don't feature a hunter overlooking a few square miles of open Western mule deer country with several thousand dollars in optics, it didn't receive a lot of fanfare. However, I did receive a letter from one man from coastal Washington. He was a blacktail hunter. Big coastal blacktails live as many of our big Western mule deer do – in the cover – and killing them requires that a hunter learn to hunt the thick and nasty. His letter simply said, "I really enjoyed your article, it was like a breath of fresh air," then listed his telephone number. I dialed the number immediately.

A genteel man on the other end of the phone answered. By his voice, I could tell he was elderly. I told him I'd received his letter and wondered what he meant by "a breath of fresh air." He said he'd spent 60 years hunting big blacktails in the coastal jungles of Washington and Oregon where you can kill them only by hunting in the cover. He'd killed over 30 big blacktails (an incredible feat), most of them from under 100 yards and many under 20 yards – and if I remember right, his rifle was open-sighted. He said he thought that today's generation was losing that skill (and the respect for that skill) of killing big bucks up close. When he read my article, he'd found some hope that those skills haven't died and was thrilled to see a writer going against the grain and expounding on the techniques to hunt in the cover. I told him his letter was like a breath of fresh air to me, too, and thanked him for writing me. I wish I could sit and drink coffee with that fellow for a few hours – oh the stories he could tell and the things I could learn!

The following nine techniques are best applied in and around the cover, not the wide open country we see in so many mule deer images. After all, unless you have a premium tag with few hunters afield, the cover is where many of the big deer will be after opening day, especially on firearms hunts. If you can learn to apply these techniques up close, then applying them in open country will be a breeze.

RECOGNIZING BUCK COUNTRY

This section could have also fit into "Small Picture Research," but I placed it here as I believe recognizing buck country is actually a technique that you must practice day by day on the hunt, not just in researching places to hunt.

When you consider behavior, big mule deer are a sub-set of the species. This is evident in the country they choose to live in. They don't just wander aimlessly like younger and less experienced bucks. Rather, I believe they choose the country they spend the most time in according to several factors – primarily feed and security – and you can develop your skill at recognizing buck country. I estimate only about 10-20 percent of a given unit holds the kind of buck you're looking for, and the ability to find that country quickly improves your odds of taking a great buck. In this chapter, I'll help you refine your skills at finding buck country, but ultimately it will be your time in the field that drives it all home.

SECURITY

I list this first because I think it is the number one factor influencing a big mule deer's behavior. If he's made it to four years old, he's encountered many dangers that have taught him how to survive. From the first day of birth, predators such as coyotes and lions (and even eagles and hawks) have been a threat. These same predators continue to follow the buck as he grows to maturity and are the reason big mule deer are difficult to track – they're always aware of danger from behind. Now consider a buck living in a hunted population. If he makes it through his first several seasons, he learns that the open country is where the danger is, as today's modern rifleman can reach out farther than ever before. Yet the thick brush and timber are mostly void of humans, so he spends his days there during the season. Also, he learns that the rough steep country gives him certain advantages – the ability to see long distances, monitor finicky thermals, and make quick escapes. A hunted big mule deer will always be in the most secure places he can find. This is why some bucks choose to live in city limits where hunting and shooting is banned. These huge bucks are saying, "I know I'm safer here than on the mountain!"

The open tops of those pretty mountains are where the hunters are. The lower thick brushy country is where the big bucks spend their season.

In almost all the places I've killed big deer, they were in country that featured varied terrain. On a topo map, that means the contour lines will be wavy and close together. There are some foothills just a few miles east of my house. Most of the hills are "smooth" with few gullies, draws, and rimrock and are pretty much devoid of bucks. However, if I spend a few hours around the rougher country, I almost always find bucks or at least buck sign. This is a truism I've seen across the West in every place that mule deer inhabit.

This photo, taken from a plane, shows an open mountainside that is steep enough to provide protection from predators – except the modern rifleman. I wouldn't expect to see big bucks here after opening day of the rifle season unless tag numbers were very low.

This photo shows the type of high-country feed that big bucks seek out in the early season before the frost.

181

QUALITY FEED

I've read several studies about mule deer bucks that have shown they can detect the quality of their feed. I've also noticed over the decades that I find big mule deer living in areas with ample feed. Even in extremely rough high country where most of the ground is covered with rock, the bucks will be where there is ample feed. Whenever I scout desert country for bucks, I look around any agricultural land in the area, because that is where most bucks seem to show up – they know where the good groceries are.

If there's no agricultural activity in the area, I still find the biggest bucks where the best feed is growing – like the north-facing rim of a rocky mesa where the feed is still green, or in an area with seven-foot-tall sagebrush (which also provides security) and ample browse. On Conservation Reserve Program (CRP) lands where farmers are paid to not grow crops, it seems after a few years, the big bucks don't feed in it much, but rather seek out newer growth like alfalfa, or an aspen stand that is not overly mature.

In areas with overly mature CRP crops, deer will seek out their native cover. Look close, at far right there's a big buck courting those does well away from the CRP field in the background.

In dry areas, I include water in the feed factor. Bucks have to drink every few days (although there is some evidence that deer in areas with no open water get all their moisture from plants), and usually live within about a mile of water and feed. You won't catch me claiming I know all the names of the forbs and plants they eat – but the bucks don't know the names either.

By recognizing country with both security and feed, you can narrow down the best places to scout and hunt. Remember that only a small percentage of your unit will hold good bucks, so you have to find these small areas.

These areas change according to season, rut, and weather, but even when the bucks are on the move, they seek out certain places.

This high country has the right mix of timber, feed, and open country – just what big bucks prefer.

The country in the foreground is where you'll find the bucks. The big mountain in the background is too rocky and low on feed for big bucks to spend much time there.

This country won't hold many big bucks once the pressure mounts
as it's too open. Any big buck here would be hiding in the
brushy draws in the center of the photo.

This country has enough brush to hide a few big bucks all season long.
I've seen several over 200 inches here and killed one.

MOVING IN DEER COUNTRY

I LEFT MY BACKCOUNTRY CAMP on my saddlehorse Rain one October morning in the pitch dark. The country I wanted to hunt was nearly two hours away. I had to be there by first light, or the bucks would be in the timber before I could cover all the country I needed to.

Two hours later, I was shivering as I climbed off Rain. I tied her a few hundred yards back in the timber and on the opposite side of the mountain from where I planned to hunt. A lone horse tends to whinny, which would alert every buck within earshot. The sky was bright in the east by now and I could see a few hundred yards. I pussyfooted out to a sharp ridge that overlooked a small brushy basin where I'd seen a few bucks over the years. It was a relatively small place covering maybe thirty acres of mountainside. There was better buck country about a half-mile farther up the mountain, but I've learned that when moving in deer country, you need to approach all likely areas with caution and in silence. That means traveling on foot and moving slowly. Riding a clomping saddlehorse close to where bucks might be is about as smart as sighting in your rifle on opening morning at sunrise.

I slowly made my way along the ridge, glassing into the occasional openings in the brush below. Snow had fallen about a week before and what remained was frozen and very crunchy, slowing me down even more. I really wanted to hurry, as I didn't expect to see a buck in this place and wanted to get to the country farther up the mountain before the sun had been up too long. But I've learned the hard way not to rush, so I stuck to my slow pace.

It was October 29, and I expected the bigger bucks to be near the does around daylight. When I spotted a small group of does at the bottom of the basin, my heart raced a little faster. I sat in the frozen snow and started glassing. The does were about 500 yards out in a brushy draw. Suddenly at the head of the draw I saw a glimpse of heavy antlers with a few cheaters. I recognized those antlers as belonging to a buck that I'd passed up earlier in the fall. Because the season closed in a few days, he was now looking pretty good. I wanted to get closer, but with all the crunchy snow and a herd of does in sight, I knew I couldn't. I tried to lie down but the vegetation in front of me blocked my view. I'd have to shoot from a sitting position so I tied a rope around my knees to steady myself for a shot that would be well over 400 yards.

It took nearly five minutes for the buck to clear the brush where I could get a shot. He was leaving the does and headed for the timber at a fast walk. Putting the crosshairs on his shoulder, I waited for him to stop. Not 20 yards from the trees, he did. I struggled to steady the crosshairs as I squeezed the trigger. He went down but was back up in an instant. I fired again just as he reached the timber. This time he went down and stayed down.

Making my way downslope to him, I found he was indeed the buck I'd passed up earlier in the year after tracking him up a steep ridge less than a mile from here. He was huge in the body and his antlers were heavy and tall with a few extra points. Had I not been moving quietly and carefully, I never would have seen that buck. He or the does would have heard my approach and darted into the cover.

By the grace of God I've hunted mule deer every year – save one – since about 1977. Those thousands of days spent in deer country have taught me one important lesson: A human moving at normal pace is completely foreign to the rhythm of the forest. Mule deer, the most keen of animals, can pick us out like a tuba in the Rose Parade.

Our very mannerisms – how we walk, turn our heads, swing our arms, and even breathe – are like big warning signs to older, experienced mule deer. It's my opinion that older bucks rarely stray from the cover in most hunted units and to kill them, you have to get closer. To get closer, you have to overcome their incredible (but vulnerable) visual and auditory senses. You have to learn how to move undetected in mule deer country. How you move actually is a technique and thus it's in this section of the book. Every other technique I write about is affected by how you move. If you don't believe that, go to the forest and pay little attention to how you move, and see how many big bucks you kill. It won't be many. Still hunting, covered in a later chapter, relies heavily on how you move, but it's a technique in and of itself. When still hunting, you focus on small pieces of cover and country known to hold bucks. However, there will be a lot of country you'll move through without still hunting, either because you're not sure there are bucks there or because you're headed for somewhere you think is better. I've killed a fair number of big deer in unlikely country that I wasn't necessarily still hunting, but I was moving carefully enough to get the drop on a big buck before he could get away. Now you might be yawning at the thought of a chapter on how to move in mule deer country. Thirty years ago, I would have too. However, with thousands of days, hundreds of spooked bucks (and dozens of big dead bucks) under my belt, I know better. How you move will determine your deadliness.

I'm Type-A personality, was a diagnosed hyperactive child (the term used before ADHD), and still live life at a whirlwind pace. For me to slow down in mule deer country has been a 25-year endeavor and I'm still learning. Writing this, I took a stroll back in my mind over the last 20 seasons. In just a few minutes, I remembered at least a dozen great-to-giant bucks that got away because I moved too fast, including one Idaho buck – a 35" heavy-monster that I had at less than 50 yards. Most of these bucks were within 100 yards and would have been chip shots had I moved slower. I've got a long way to go. However I'm confident, if only because of my failures, that I can help you kill more big deer by convincing you to move slower in mule deer country.

A mule deer's vision is designed to see movement. A human has a 180-degree field of view; with a mule deer's 310-degree field of view, there is only a small slot behind their heads where they can't see. However, they struggle to identify stationary objects, especially if the object is obscured and not skylined. That is the chink in their armor.

Their hearing is also incredible and greatly underestimated by hunters. Cup your hands behind your ears and notice how much sound is magnified. Now imagine if you had their funnel-shaped 9-inch ears swiveling in every direction like some radar station. Deer can also hear at a much wider frequency than humans. They react to noise we aren't even aware of, especially high-frequency noise like a metal zipper touching against a rifle barrel. The only way to overcome these senses is to move slowly.

I've spent years trying to figure out how much movement I can get away with around mule deer. My conclusion? Not very much. If you are in open country, moving more than 100 yards per hour (0.06 mph) is a dead giveaway to mule deer within 200 yards. If you can see the deer and time your movement right, you can move a little faster – but not much. If you're in thick cover, you have to be closer to 50 yards an hour (0.03 mph)! These paces are painstakingly tough to maintain. I have to be confident I'm near deer to keep this pace, and it's why I pay close attention to tracks and try to hunt areas I know very well. Then I know where I have to move slowly and where I don't.

The speed of body movement, not just walking speed, must also be controlled. In civilization, if we hear a sound, we turn our heads toward it. In deer country, that simple movement done at normal speed can alert deer. Even bringing your binoculars to your eyes at normal speed is enough to spook nearby deer. I could go on, but you should be getting the point – you must control all body movement in the arms, torso, and head, both to overcome their visual sense for movement and to make less noise.

By moving slowly, you are also much better able to control sound. Most of us only worry about breaking sticks, kicking rocks, and wearing quiet clothing, but you have to be even more careful. Your arms brushing against your torso, your frozen pant-cuffs touching each other, your weapon contacting small branches, coughing, spitting, sniffing – everything has to be considered. Slow movement lessens the frequency and intensity of unwanted sounds. Mule deer are specifically and intimately familiar with all the "normal" sounds of safety in their environment, and a zipper clanging on a rifle barrel is not one of those sounds. By controlling your sounds, bucks can become vulnerable.

I've hunted with and studied quite a few very good deer hunters in my life. While they all had their own hunting styles, I've learned the same thing from all of them: hunt slow. While each of these men (and one woman) taught me bookfuls, my best teacher has actually been my quarry: older, experienced mule deer bucks. Study these masters of movement and I guarantee your mule deer game will improve dramatically.

Except for a few days in the peak of the rut, or if he's spooked, a big buck will move very deliberately. Before moving, he'll thoroughly survey his surroundings. Once everything looks safe, he'll walk a few steps, stop for a few seconds to a few minutes, and repeat the whole cycle again. This is why he rarely walks into danger. He's very aware of his surroundings.

Watch a bachelor herd of bucks feeding. You'll notice the older bucks move less and move more slowly than their younger, less experienced counterparts. What you're witnessing is the fact that older, bigger bucks move very deliberately. We must imitate them if we want to kill more big mule deer.

Here are some situations where we spook bucks:

- ☐ You've glassed quietly for two hours with no luck. You stand up quickly and saunter over to your pack leaned against a tree and start rifling through it. Any big buck that drifted into range while you were glassing will easily pick out that ruckus and simply fade back into the cover, often without your ever knowing he was there. Rather, stand up slowly and don't take any steps. Survey your surroundings, both with the naked eye (wide angle view) and with your binoculars. Then slowly walk to your pack and try not to make any unnecessary noise. You've just invested two hours into the perfect ambush situation, so don't screw it up now.

- ☐ You and your buddy are pulling the steepest hill of the hunt. It's so steep, you've forgotten all about being quiet and just want to survive so you can get to the top to glass. You sound like a rutting rhino as you step over brush, kick rocks, and poke fun at your chubby buddy falling behind. Every buck within a half-mile can hear this fiasco, and it will put them on high alert.

Big bucks are rarely where we think they are, and that's why we need to hunt quietly any time we are in deer country. Always give yourself more time to reach your destination so you're not forced to walk quickly and noisily, especially if no one else is spooking the deer. I've killed several good bucks in surprise places I was only walking through to get where I thought I should be. I was still moving carefully, though, so I was able to put one in the boiler room before they made their escape.

Another good buck I killed unexpectedly as
I moved through some likely buck country.

Many hunters walk into deer country falsely thinking that if they spook a big buck, he'll expose himself and the hunter can shoot him. That era ended about 1965. A big mule deer buck, when spooked, will put every bush, tree, rock, and terrain feature between himself and a hunter in a matter of seconds as he makes his escape. If you are hunting for a big mule deer by just walking through deer country, give up while you still have knee cartilage left. Few big bucks fall for that trick.

I don't want to sound like I'm some phantom drifting undetected like smoke among the forest creatures. I'm a bumbling human being who also has a hard time leaving the pace of life behind. But sometimes, some days, I hit it just right – often for reasons I can't explain. My brain and body began to work together in a calmness that allows me to move very slowly and very quietly, just like big bucks move. While I don't kill a big deer every time I move slowly, I've killed virtually all of my big deer when I'm moving slowly. You will, too.

You can't just show up in deer country and live the pace of life like we do in civilization. You should move in a way that you see deer before they detect you, virtually every time. Next time you're around deer – any deer – slow down everything. I think you'll begin to see what I mean.

OBEYING THE WIND

Obey: to comply with or follow the commands, restrictions, wishes, or instructions of.

Years ago, I paid attention to the wind only on a stalk. That is like an elk hunter who considers the wind only after a bull answers. Both strategies are flawed. I've learned that I must obey the wind long before I even see a deer. By obeying, I mean I let the wind decide how I'm going to hunt a certain area.

I've written about the incredible defense a mule deer buck's giant ears offer him. I suggest that his nose is just as formidable an opponent. Many a great buck has escaped me because of his nose. Just two years ago, I sneaked within 18 yards of a 200+" bedded buck I'd affectionately dubbed Jalapeño because he was such a "hot" looking buck. I had his escape route covered and all day for him to stand and feed a bit – he was as good as dead. But, just as too many times before, it was the wind that gave him the tip that I was there. Watching him bound to safety felt as good as three root canals in one day. For every buck I know that winded me, I'd bet that five escaped without my ever knowing they existed.

Some biologists estimate that a mule deer's sense of smell is up to 1,000 times stronger than a human's. Research suggests that a mule deer can detect human odor at up to a half mile away and I believe it.

One evening a few years back, hunting in Idaho's high country, I spotted a 180-class buck feeding on a bench below an avalanche chute. With the wind in my face, I quickly moved within 450 yards and set up. As I looked him over deciding whether I was going to punch my tag, I felt the breeze shift toward him. Within seconds, he slowly lifted his head, and put his nose to the wind. Without hesitation, he disappeared into the timber ... forever.

Deer constantly monitor the wind. They lick their noses to keep them moist, which helps odor particles stick, further improving their sense of smell. I believe a big buck will move with the wind at his tail only if he's certain no danger lies ahead. More often I see them moving into the wind, doubling their ability to sense danger before it's too late. A big buck will bed in a place where the prevailing wind is finicky and changes directions frequently. It's a survival technique they learned as babies that they continue to hone over the years.

Remote high country is most challenging because deer there rarely smell humans. One whiff of a man and they are gone, often for the season. That is the problem with just a few guys hunting sloppily in high country. They can completely ruin an entire drainage by not obeying the wind and moving wrong. Smaller, less experienced bucks will stick around, giving the illusion that the big ones are close by, but they aren't. The scent of a hunter drifting down the basin in the pre-dawn darkness sent those big deer into the timber long before first light.

In lower, thicker country, I've seen good bucks live within 600 yards of a road for the entire hunting season. These bucks are accustomed to human scent. They don't freak out and change drainages like a high-country buck. A big buck living where humans are common will simply move slowly away from the scent of a hunter, or hold tight until the hunter passes. Unless you see his tracks, or he blows out when he smells you, you'll never know he was close.

If I've scouted and know there is a good buck around, I never let my scent blow into the area until I know where he's hiding. I glass, track, ambush, and still-hunt with the wind in my face until I've got him pegged. If I don't know where a buck is spending his time, I try to guess before getting within a half-mile of the area, so I don't pollute the area with my scent. With either scenario, I might not move more than a few hundred yards in a morning if I think there are bucks around. The average hunters I meet cover that much ground in five minutes, and it's why they rarely kill bucks more than two or three years old. While scent eliminating products seem to work well for stationary whitetail hunters, I don't bother with it in mule deer country where I'm hunting on foot. I'm too sweaty and simply don't have the time or patience or money to have a fresh set of unscented hunting clothes ready for each day. Even more important, I've learned (and am still learning) that all I need to do is obey the wind!

This six-year old (lab-aged) Colorado buck weighed nearly 400 pounds on the hoof. I took him in a small oakbrush-choked basin where I've seen many a good buck. There is no way to hunt the basin until you are within about 300 yards, so I always approach it with the wind in my face. After sneaking in there before sun-up one morning with a friend, I took a stand and watched the heavy cover. Not an hour later, this buck appeared for a few seconds in a small opening in the oakbrush jungle below. Had we not paid attention to the wind, I would have never seen him.

Now that I've covered hunting slowly and the importance of considering the wind, we can better consider the other techniques. It doesn't matter if you're spot-and-stalk hunting, tracking, or ambush hunting – if you don't pay attention to the wind and how you move, you'll struggle to kill big smart bucks.

STILL-HUNTING

WHEN I FIRST HEARD THE TERM STILL-HUNTING as a teenager, I thought it meant "being still while hunting" and I find that many hunters think the same thing. That definition is actually better suited to ambush hunting, which I'll cover later. Here is the Robby Denning definition:

Still-hunting: hunting slowly through an area known to or thought to hold the target species when no other technique will work.

I put a lot of thought into that definition and believe it captures the essence and purpose of still-hunting. First, hunting slowly is the only way to overcome a big buck's senses when you're forced into the cover where many spend their time after opening day.

Second, the definition considers where to apply the technique. That is a key concept if you're going to be effective at still-hunting. You can't just randomly still-hunt through the forest. Still-hunting is a game of concentration and focus and your effective time is limited – and it's very tiring. Physically, it's not too tough, as you're moving slowly, but it is hard (especially for a hyper person like me) mentally because of the concentration and focus it takes. Therefore, my definition includes the "where" to apply still hunting: "an area

known or thought to hold the target species."

I apply still-hunting where I've seen good bucks or their sign. Big bucks do not just randomly wander the countryside; they stick to relatively small core areas with the right cover, feed, and security most of the time. These areas are usually smaller than a square mile and often just a few hundred acres, so they can be hunted in a half-day or so. Once I find those places, the stalker in me comes out and I still-hunt. However, these places need to be small enough that I can apply still-hunting effectively. You can't (at least I can't) still-hunt effectively for ten hours; I'm good for about three hours. After that, I have a hard time maintaining focus and I start making mistakes like moving too fast or spacing out, and my vision starts to wander. I start spooking bucks when I'm not focused, polluting my area.

Still hunting some thick cover in southeast Utah.

Finally, my definition specifies when to still-hunt: "when other techniques won't work." Glassing is very effective, but there are many big-buck hideouts where glassing is nearly impossible. Tracking is one of my favorite techniques, but in the hard rocky soil of the Intermountain West where I hunt the most, unless you have snow, it's hard to track a buck more than a few hundred yards. Also, even when you have snow, there's usually only a small window of days where the conditions allow you to track. Frozen crunchy snow is like tracking in potato chips and it's very hard to get close to a buck. Ambush hunting is a deadly technique but is hard to do when the weather is cold and you can't sit long. That leaves still-hunting as your preferred technique when the others aren't working.

Most big deer hunters I talk to don't like still-hunting. They'd rather play the optics game and only stalk the bucks they've already pegged. That is a great way to hunt, but big mule deer living in units with much hunting pressure at all (which is where you'll spend most of your time as those are the units where you can get a tag), the biggest bucks don't live in places where only glassing will be effective.

I've met hunters who hunted some great open high country like Wyoming's Hoback Range or Colorado's San Juan Mountains before many people hunted those places. Back then, you had a legitimate chance of killing a big mule deer by simply glassing until you found a stalkable buck. Hunt those places now and all you'll see are hunters spooking bucks into the timber. There are enough hunters that someone's going to kill a big one, making you think if you just glass a little longer and harder, you will too. Unless it's a draw hunt with few tags, that is mostly a farce (for big mule deer.) For someone trying to kill one on purpose, glassing alone won't produce much. You have to go where the big ones are, and the only way to hunt those places without tracking snow is to still-hunt the cover.

One year with my friend Trevor Carlson, I hunted a thick Montana mountain range where a few giant bucks had been killed in recent years. When I saw the mountain range for the first time, I knew exactly why giant mule deer lived there. Rather than the big beautiful green mountain basins so common in the kill pictures in the magazines, it was densely forested, with only a few hundred acres of open ridgetops in each drainage. Because it wasn't glassable country, I saw zero hunters once I left the road.

As we penetrated the country over the course of a week, I'd find small areas of broken cover where the sun could reach the ground and stimulate growth of the forbs and herbs that deer prefer, and that was where I'd find the deer. Still, there was so much timber, I couldn't glass more than a few hundred yards at most. My spotting scope was about worthless. It was late November, the heat of the rut, and I was finding enough does to give me hope. But I'd seen no bucks in a week of hard hunting. I did, however, see more than a few big blocky tracks and fresh rubs in those areas, so I knew there were big bucks around. They were just spending daylight hours in the cover. Who says big mule deer are dumb in the rut?

The snow had been on the ground for weeks and was very crunchy, so tracking bucks was proving fruitless. On the seventh day, I decided to focus on still-hunting an area where I'd seen multiple tracks, rubs, and other fresh sign.

Not long after daylight, Trevor and I tied our horses in one of the few openings so we'd have a good chance of finding them later without having to backtrack. I headed west toward the cover while Trevor headed east to hunt some country that was a bit more open – which is a relative term in that unit.

My first hour, I hunted slowly and covered a few hundred yards, making sure I understood how to use the prevailing wind. I cut several smokin' hot tracks and a few were big, but I'd yet to see any deer. It was below 20 degrees, so I couldn't move too slowly or I'd get cold. By hour two, I was in the groove of still-hunting and was able to move slowly and quietly enough that I knew I had a chance at seeing a buck before he saw me, especially if he was on his feet. By the date on the calendar, November 23, I knew bucks could move at any hour of the day. I could never see more than 100 yards and often it was more like 50. The number of fresh rubs kept me encouraged, though, and the fact that there were rubs of various ages dating back decades told me I was in a traditional rutting area – a really golden find.

I kept this pace up – or down, to be accurate – until around noon and had covered less than a mile when my stomach reminded me it had been nearly eight hours since breakfast. I found a bench in the timber that allowed me to look over a steep timbered slope below me with about 100 yards of visibility. I quietly dug out the snow below a big lodgepole pine and sat against the trunk with my rifle in reach. I pulled out a peanut butter and jelly sandwich and settled in. The forest was dark, cold, and a little unfriendly, but my hopes were high as I had been so careful to hunt the area, I had the wind, and there was plenty of fresh sign.

I was almost done with my sandwich and had a bite of it in my mouth when out of my left eye, I caught movement about 70 yards below me. I grabbed my rifle and scanned the slope through my scope. I caught movement again and saw a behemoth-chested buck step from behind a tree into an opening only wide enough to expose his head and chest. I glanced at the antlers and could see he was heavy, so I dropped and pulled at the same instant he was about to take another step. He bucked and kicked then spun and ran downslope. I jacked another shell in the chamber, but he was gone. Seconds later, I heard a crash so loud I thought a tree had fallen – and then the forest fell silent. I finished chewing the bite of sandwich still in my mouth, retrieved the dropped crust from the snow, and gathered my pack.

I found where the bullet had cut hair and left a spray of blood on the snow. He was hit hard but I took up the track just as if he were unwounded, rifle ready. About 20 yards down the slope, I could see where he'd dived through an old blowdown that was held up at a 45-degree angle by its massive branches impaled into the ground. There were several branches as big as a man's forearm busted off clean where the buck had blown through the tangle

201

as he made his escape. On the other side of the blowdown, I could see he'd lost his footing on the steep slope and had slid down the mountain out of sight into a heavy tangle of alders. I had to sidehill my way down, it was so steep and slick. Once in the alders, I found the buck sidled up to a big log and dead as a rock. His antlers were heavy and dark, his body nearly twice the size of the few deer I'd seen in the previous week of hunting. His hooves were big and he smelled heavily of the rut.

As I glanced around the forest, I couldn't see more than about 70 yards in any direction. I knew that had I not been still-hunting correctly, I'd never have even seen this buck, let alone put a bullet where it counted in the few seconds he gave me.

AMBUSH HUNTING

Ambush: an act or instance of lying concealed so as to attack by surprise.

One thing that draws me to mule deer hunting is that no matter how much you learn or how much you succeed, you've never arrived. There are so many levels to becoming a great mule deer hunter that you must never quit learning. If you do, you'll stagnate and become bored with the pursuit. You won't be able to push through the hard times, because there is nothing calling you on. "Been there, done that" will be your attitude, and sitting in a warm truck will win out over climbing a slick steep slope in the dark. You'll think you're just getting old, but it's more likely that you've just quit learning.

When I was younger, I zipped from peak to peak, canyon to canyon, knob to knob like my pants were on fire. I was always in a hurry to get things done (sometimes, I still am). Oh, I killed some big mule deer but looking back, they had made mistakes – like letting me see where they bedded or staying out of the cover just a little too long after sunrise. Big bucks were still getting away if the entire onus was on me to get it done. I needed to come up with more ways to kill big deer than by simply hunting my guts out hoping a big buck would blunder into range.

I was starting to learn that some bucks can be killed only by slowing down to a dead stop. In many places, the cover was too thick or the conditions wouldn't allow for other methods like spot-and-stalk, still-hunting, or tracking; I had to let the deer come to me by setting an ambush where I thought they'd eventually show up.

By ambush hunting, I don't mean ambushing a buck that you've bedded as he gets up to stretch or feed – by definition, that is spot-and-stalk hunting because you knew pretty much where he was. By ambush hunting, I'm talking about lying in wait for a buck or bucks you only *suspect* are there based on previous sightings, tracks, or rubs – and/or trails or terrain features that might predict where your quarry will show up. Basically you're relying on an educated guess and your own patience to succeed. This is why ambush hunting isn't all that popular but is still the only way to kill some bucks. It's also a very very satisfying experience when it all comes together.

Avalanche chutes with plenty of timber are
prime places to ambush big mule deer.

I've met some relatively inexperienced hunters who've tagged some really big bucks by ambush hunting. I think they're successful in part because they're not comfortable yet at tracking, glassing, or still-hunting, but plopping down on a stump for a few hours to watch the deer country just makes sense to them. Other hunters, even the experienced, continue to tromp around spreading their scent and noise through mule deer kingdom and rarely kill a big mule deer on purpose. A hunter with a broken silhouette sitting motionless with the wind in his favor is almost undetectable by even the wiliest of big bucks.

In 2003 the West had seen a series of six mild winters. It had been 10 years since the infamous winterkill of 1992-93 and I was starting to see some pretty good bucks showing up in the country I knew well in Idaho, Wyoming, and Colorado. That October, I planned a nine-day solo hunt in some Idaho backcountry where I'd seen a few great bucks over the years. The general season opened October 5 back then, and I was on the mountain by dawn of October 2 glassing some of my favorite buck country. One place I used to hunt allowed me to sit on one ridge and glass a 4½-mile circle where I could see at least four bucky places with the rising sun at my back. I was using a pair of 16x50 Pentax tripod-mounted binoculars to peer into each of the honey holes.

It was about 9:00 a.m. and I'd seen a few deer scattered about, but nothing that looked big. Glassing at several miles or more, you're not counting inches of antler but rather looking for other clues including body size, behavior, and the occasional glint of a sunray reflecting from a big antler to confirm buck sightings. From there, you have to use your head to devise a plan to hunt any bucks you think are worth pursuing. As I turned the tripod around to check once more a mountainside three miles distant, I saw two deer facing each other in the bright sunlight at timber's edge. By body size and the rough terrain, I figured they were bucks. Soon they were head-to-head shoving each other around in the open sagebrush, so I knew they were sparring antlers. I don't see the big bucks spar until the November rut, so I figured they weren't more than about three years old, but I continued to watch anyway.

After a few minutes, they quit sparring and started moving toward the timber. Right then I picked up a third deer that had probably been there the whole time but hadn't been moving, so I'd missed him. That was my first clue he was likely an older buck – they don't move as much as their younger cohorts. This buck looked bigger in the body, too. As they entered the dark spruce, I could easily see the antlers of the third deer contrasted for a brief second against the dark background. While I wasn't sure how big he was, he certainly had enough bone to keep me interested. The other two bucks' antlers didn't even show up at that distance. It would take a half day on horseback to get to that mountain and another half day to reset camp, so I elected to continue to hunt a few days in some of the closer country and see if I could turn up a good buck before losing a day of hunting to check on the other buck.

During the next six days I was in buck country at all prime hours when bucks might move, and I spent a few hours during the mid-day glassing likely country. I'd seen several nice bucks, including one that was right at the 180" mark and about 26" or 27" wide, but I elected to pass and look for something bigger. I heard rifle shots occasionally in the distance but hadn't talked to a human being since I kissed Jodi goodbye nearly a week before. The moon was becoming full and a heat wave was predicted, so hunting conditions were worsening. I had to be back to work by October 10, so with only one day left to hunt, I packed camp, saddled and loaded the horses, and headed for the mountainside I'd seen the bucks on nearly a week before.

I knew there had surely been hunters there since the opener, but those bucks were living on a slope that could be hunted only by still-hunting in quiet conditions or by ambush hunting. There was really nowhere to glass the slope until you were right on top of it. I'd learned over the years that big bucks like places like that, because the average hunter (and I!) tromp along like a rutting moose looking for places we can sit and glass for hours, all the while sending bucks into the cover with our noise and scent. Anyone hunting that slope would likely spend about five minutes glassing the few openings and then move on to more open country.

By the evening of October 8, I had camp set back up as the sun sank toward the western horizon. I don't camp where I can spook deer, so I was still an hour from the deer country and had sacrificed an evening to hunt the bucks I'd only glimpsed from three miles away. I just went to bed early, tired from the long week of hunting.

The next morning, I rose well before 4:00, broke camp under a stunning full moon, and loaded the horses. I was in the saddle by 6:00 a.m. with a plan to just hunt the morning then head out to the truck from there. I climbed the mountain trail as the eastern horizon began to show a hue of light. The horses knew we were going home and had a renewed vigor I hadn't seen in days. I tied them off before 7:00 a.m. in a small patch of windblown spruce about a mile from the hillside I'd seen the bucks on.

I walked as quietly as possible through the crunchy sage as dawn competed with the still-bright moon. I could see fresh boot tracks in several places where hunters had searched the open country during the previous week. I knew if I stopped to glass the open basins, I'd probably see bucks, but they'd be younger than three. The big boys would have retreated to the timber with all the hunting.

As the sun crested the mountains to the east, I sat hidden in a big boulder pile above the slope where I'd seen the bucks. I'd marked out some features in my mind when I'd first glassed the bucks the week before – like certain trees and rocks – and figured I was sitting about 100 yards from where I'd seen them. My little weather radio had forecasted record highs for the day – near 90 in the valleys – and sure enough, I didn't even need a coat at this early hour when temps are usually below freezing.

To my left were some open sagebrush ridges. Below me was broken timber and brush with visibility to about 150 yards. To the right, the timber became thicker and I could see only a few scattered openings the size of a car out to about 200 yards, then no visibility beyond that. Part of me felt like I needed to be where I could see more country, especially at this time of the morning when bucks are so active, but I knew better so I stayed put.

After an hour, the air was heating rapidly and I'd seen no animals save a few chipmunks and birds. It was now late enough that moving anywhere else would be even more futile, so I committed to sitting another hour before making my way back to the horses. I thought about the previous week hunting alone in the backcountry. I'd seen a dozen or more nice bucks – including a real tempter – and had thoroughly enjoyed the horses and camp. Going home without a buck stung a little, but there was a part of my heart that knew I'd made some memories to last a lifetime.

Something moved in the timber below, shaking me from my thoughts. I pulled the binocs up and saw a nice four-point standing at timber's edge, hard to see in the heavy shadows. He moved cautiously a few yards out of the cover and began feeding. Within a few minutes, a three-point joined him. The range was less than 150 yards. I checked to make sure my rifle was still within reach. Soon the two bucks squared off for a shoving match just like the week before. I was enjoying the show through my glass and even noticed that the four-point had a nearly five-inch cheater growing from the junction of his G2-G3. He was a young buck – probably three – but certainly had the genetics to be something special if he made it a few more years.

I kept checking the timber where the bucks had emerged. About the fourth time I looked, there was a third buck! Instantly I could see that he was much bigger in the body than the other two, but he was broadside so I couldn't tell much about his antlers. I lowered the binoculars and slowly reached for my Weatherby. I peered through the binocs again, just as the buck slowly turned and looked quartering uphill toward my left. I could see a wide frame plus twin cheaters on each G-3 putting him over 35". I brought the rifle to my shoulder and aimed low to compensate for the steep slope.

The first shot hit home, causing him to crouch low at the impact but then spin and run. I already had a shell in the chamber and held on the back of his neck as he attempted an escape. The knockdown power of a 7-mag at under 150 yards was evident as the bullet struck between his shoulder blades, spinning him around 180 degrees before he hit the dirt like a sack of cement.

Checking my watch, it wasn't even 9:00 a.m. yet. I made my way down to him and was struck with how wide he was. I pulled a quarter-inch steel tape from my pack and stretched it across the antlers – 36 inches. I looked east and scanned the country until my eyes found the ridge from where I'd first spotted the bucks – nearly three miles away and a week earlier. I was sure this was the third buck I'd seen for just a few seconds that morning. Had I not set an ambush, I'd never have taken him in the warm dry conditions. A few hours later, I had him loaded on the horses and was headed out of the backcountry, still shocked at what had happened in the waning moments of a nine-day hunt. I praised the God of heaven.

I killed this nine-year old Idaho buck by ambush.
He's the oldest buck I've ever taken.

Since that day, I've killed several more big mule deer by ambush, including my best typical. While ambush hunting is not my first choice in techniques, it is one of the most effective (and satisfying) ways to kill a big deer. Study your quarry, study your area, and if you think an ambush might work, give it a shot. You might just kill the biggest buck of your life.

Another good buck I took by ambush hunting.

Steep rolling hillsides make glassing bucks within rifle range very difficult. If there is good sign in the area, try an ambush at daylight or dusk. You might be surprised at what shows up.

TRACKING

Hunting for big mule deer is both science and art. No hunting technique for big mule deer is more a mix of these two than tracking. There is the science of the track – the dimensions and characteristics that indicate a big buck – and there is the observation and understanding of all the conditions that affect your ability to track, including snow, rain, temperature, humidity, soil type, wind, and more. The art comes in when you start making decisions based on what you observe. Whether you think the buck leaving those tracks is in a hurry so you'd better be also, or if he seems to be ready to bed and it's time for you to slow down, way down, you have decisions to make based on your observations. Will this track lead you below the ridge into the timber or will the buck cross that open ridge, giving you a shot?

I think tracking skill is essential to the big mule deer hunter, so much so that I've spent the last 25 years learning all I could about the pursuit. The more I've learned and practiced tracking, the more successful I've become at finding big mule deer. One hunt from about eight years back fondly comes to mind.

I slid down from the saddle and tied my horse, Rain, to a big blowdown. Walking back about 15 yards down the scant horse trail, I found the lone set of tracks that had caught my eye from horseback. The buck had crossed the trail in a pinch-point where one stand of timber ended on the left of the trail and another stand began on the right. Had he crossed 50 yards sooner or later, he'd have been in the open.

His track was big – over 3 inches long – but it was blocky and blunt, the first indication that he was a big buck. The rear lobes of his front track sank deeper than the rest of his track. This buck probably weighed over 250 pounds. His stride looked to be about 25" or 26" long between tracks – another clue this was no three-year-old buck. Backtracking into the broken timber, I found a fresh bed 20 yards off the trail. It seemed the buck had been bedded at this early hour of the day but had heard Rain and me coming up the trail, and made his exit into the thick timber of the mountain's northwest slope.

It had snowed overnight, and more was forecast. If I wanted to take a look at this buck's antlers, I needed to get right on his track before he put too much vertical real estate between us. I stripped down to my wool shirt despite the 20-degree temps and pending storm.

For the first 300 yards, I stayed right in his tracks to determine his mood. Was he going to break into a run or just walk a few hundred yards from the risk of the horse trail and resume his day? The tracks stayed in a straight line but for the few places he navigated around fallen timber. In a few places, his back track stepped beyond his front track, indicating he was a little concerned with what he'd heard near the horse trail. He was losing elevation as he dropped farther down the slope.

Because I'd hunted this area before, I knew the slope gave way to a semi-timbered basin about a half-mile ahead. Timbered cliffs lined the basin's upper end on what would be my left, while the lower half of the basin was more open grassy slopes with just a few patches of snow-stunted spruce on the right. Any buck older than four probably wouldn't cross the basin in the open, so I elected to stay high and hug the cliffs.

A few hundred yards later his tracks slowed; now his rear track was printing in his front track, shrinking his stride by six inches. He even wandered left to right a bit and seemed to be settling down. The snow of the previous night had fallen on week-old snow, and I could see old track impressions under the freshly fallen snow. So could he, apparently – because at each place where he'd cross the older tracks, he'd slow or stop, as if he were trying to pick up clues on where other deer in the area were headed. In another place, farther down the mountain but still in the thick timber, several younger deer –

probably bucks – had climbed the timbered slope that morning. He considered their tracks and even followed them for 40 yards or so before abandoning them and turning west back onto his original heading.

About 200 hundred yards farther, the trees began to thin as the cliffs became visible through the treetops in front of me. I un-shouldered my rifle, checked to make sure my scope covers were operational and my safety was free. I pulled the bolt back an inch and saw the shiny brass of the live round, then locked the bolt back down. I now kept the pistol grip of the rifle in my right hand, resting on the shell-holder on my belt, distributing the weight more evenly. With this carry, I could pull the gun to my shoulder and flip the scope covers up in less than a second.

The buck's tracks slowed even more as the cover gave way to the cliffs; he seemed to be contemplating where he'd cross the basin to reach the heavy timber on the other side. I thought he'd hug the base of the cliffs as there was plenty of cover there that would make him hard to see. I moved as fast as I dared while trying to be quiet. Fresh fallen snow can still make a crunch sound as the hunter's foot rolls through the step compressing the snow, a sound a buck can easily hear at 100 yards. I was looking high toward the cliffs and paying less attention to the broken timber – it was open enough that a glance or two should show me any moving buck.

And then I saw him.

He'd been standing in the last hint of timber before the basin opened up, looking back on his track, a final check before he'd make his sprint across the open grassy slopes that I'd thought he'd avoid. He saw me and instantly turned left upslope, heading for the heavier timber below the cliffs. In a second, I'd calculated his spread as about 28" – plenty wide enough for this nimrod – but his antlers were a little light, probably four inches at the base but thinner as the beams swept away from his body.

As he entered the last opening below the cliffs at about 100 yards, my rifle was at my shoulder. As he trotted straight away, I held on the base of his neck just above his shoulder blades. I began to press the trigger but then stopped in the last second that I'd have to kill him.

As he disappeared into the timber forever, I wasn't sure whether I'd actually passed him up or I just wasn't quick enough to make the shot. Either way was okay. It was opening day, 2007 Idaho, and although he was a good buck, I had 30 days of season left and really wanted a buck with more mass. I was satisfied with my efforts and felt that if he'd had fantastic antlers, I may have got to wrap my hands around them. I also knew that I wouldn't have ever seen that buck by any method other than tracking. Even opening day, he was already using the cover and avoiding the open basins where the hunting pressure was mounting. By the time I made it back to Rain, the snow had set in hard and visibility was reduced to 100 yards.

Another half-mile up the mountain, I cut more buck tracks, these from a bachelor herd of bucks at timber's edge near the top of an open basin. It looked like they had been in the open, feeding during the night, but then had fed close to the timber by daylight. The tracks entered the cover, so I stepped out of the saddle and again tied Rain. One track looked pretty good, not quite as long as the other I'd just tracked, but still blunt. I shed my coat and heavy gloves and took up the tracks.

The bunch had hit the timber and then turned and went straight up a 45-degree slope along the rim of the basin. The rim's edge featured scattered burnt timber, and the bucks stayed in it as they headed toward the high peak above the basin. The slope was very steep and I struggled to stay upright while still keeping my eyes ahead. By the falling snow, I could see the tracks were less than a quarter-hour old, so I was ready for action at any moment.

Just below the rocky peak above, the bucks turned west and entered several hundred yards of snow-stunted spruce about six feet high. The spruce grew in strips with about 50 yards of open rocky terrain between stands. The bucks walked across the rocks, about the size of bowling balls, as elegantly as if it were a mowed lawn. As I'd near the edge of each strip, I'd stop and scan the terrain ahead out to a few hundred yards. About the third time I stopped, I saw the backline of a deer standing at the edge of a mature stand of timber about 150 yards uphill. I dropped to my knee and readied myself.

With my binoculars, I picked out five bucks scattered in a 30-yard area, some bedded, some standing. They didn't know they were being followed, as the heavily falling snow obscured my form and sound. The best buck was only about 24" wide but he was heavy at the base – over five inches – and carried it all the way to the top of his three-point main frame. He had several extra non-typical points. While he was tempting, I decided to let him pass (I actually killed him near the last day of the season – he lab-aged at 5½ years old and was one of the biggest-bodied bucks I'd taken up to that point).

I backed up into the timber until I was out of sight and then dropped back down the steep slope headed back to Rain. Huge snowflakes fell so fast that I almost didn't see her until I was within 30 yards. I donned my gloves and heavy coat over my damp wool shirt and climbed back into the saddle. The open country to the east was visible between snow squalls, but I knew the big bucks weren't there anymore. I was tired; I'd tracked nearly three miles in the steep terrain, but it was a good tired. As I headed for greener pastures down the mountain, I was thankful that I'd learned to track big bucks so many years ago – and I'm still learning. Sometimes it is the only way to find them once they've shed their velvet and left the most open country.

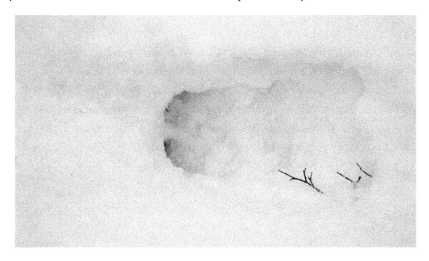

When I cut the track of a big mule deer buck, something inside me comes alive. Other than seeing a buck with my own eyes, there is no better indication I'm in the right area than finding the blocky track of a heavy-bodied buck. Tracking should be one of the top tools in a buck hunter's tool kit. My daddy was a phenomenal bear tracker and sparked my interest early on.

Depending on where in the West you're hunting mule deer, the value of tracking will vary. In the high country, tracking is important but very physically challenging. Bucks can easily leave a man in the dust in minutes, even when not spooked. A man, no matter his physical condition, can only catch up with a buck in the high country – where a buck can put eight walking-hours between himself and his tracker in 30 minutes – with the most finesse a tracker can muster. He can't spook him and then expect to catch back up for a second chance like he can on bucks living in lower and gentler country. With more rainfall in the high country, vegetation is abundant and tracks harder to see. Without snow, most bucks in this habitat are difficult to track. However, with adequate water and cover, bucks seem to have a smaller home range, so tracking jobs can be shorter.

In the sand and clay soils of the arid Southwest and the Colorado Plateau (130,000 square miles of real estate taking in western Colorado, northwest New Mexico, southern and eastern Utah, and northern Arizona) tracks are easier to follow. Ground vegetation is sparser, helping the hunter. However, in flatter and drier country, bucks seem to roam more. A hunter may need to cover 5-20 miles per day.

I've taken several of my top bucks by tracking, including my 224-2/8" Gross (official score) Wyoming buck. I found him in early August, but didn't kill him until October 4 after hunting 16 days between archery and rifle. In September, during the archery season, I'd sneaked to within 40 yards and waited for him to stand. A smaller buck noticed me peering over a rise and spooked the herd. Bucks often have identifiable track features, so I checked the big boy's bed. Here is my journal entry from that day:

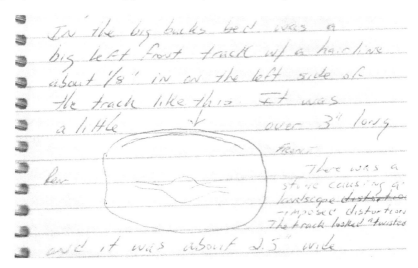

After the rifle opener, he stayed in the timbered country. The only way to narrow down where to hunt was by his track, so I scoured the mountain. On the last day, just as a blizzard was setting in, I found a track matching my journal entry. A few hours later, I made an 80-yard shot as he stood from his bed in the timber. Tracking was his undoing.

If you want to hunt and kill big mule deer, there are track characteristics and buck behaviors you must understand.

TRACK CHARACTERISTICS

Anyone who says you can't tell bucks from does by their tracks is just wrong. Bucks have wider chests and does have wider hips, and both these traits show up in their tracks if you look. If you're a big deer hunter, it's pretty easy to tell outsized bucks from other deer – it's no harder than tracking an NBA player versus a soccer player.

I've lab-aged all my big deer and can assure you that any buck with good antlers is going to be at least four years old. That means he'll also weigh between 200 and 400 pounds, far larger than other deer in the herd – and his tracks will show it. With practice, you'll notice that the buck's weight shows in his track. It will be deeper, especially toward the rear lobes of the track. With heavy bucks, their dew claws often show up in the track, when those of smaller deer don't.

Shape is a great indicator, too. Big bucks' front tracks are very blunt and nearly as wide as they are long, and rear tracks are more pointed and smaller. I've measured many over the last 20 years and virtually all of them were between 3" and 3½" long and 2¼" to 2½" wide.

These badly worn hooves are from an 8-year-old 300 lb. Idaho buck I shot. A careful tracker would be able to identify these wear patterns in a good track impression. Notice the front hooves on the left are bigger and blockier than the rear hooves.

While not as individualized as a human fingerprint, bucks also have identifying features in their tracks. Chips, cracks, irregular shapes, and other oddities are there if you look for them. Notice in my journal entry above the features I identified. A month later, the day I killed him, those same features were still visible.

STRIDE LENGTH

Just as a tall man has a longer stride than a regular guy, so does a big mule deer. Mature bucks will span 24" to 28" between tracks when walking on level ground.

The longest I've ever seen was left by a Franklin County, Idaho, buck back in 2001. That buck had a 30" stride and was surely at 350-400 lbs. I never caught up to him before the skiff of snow melted, so can only imagine his antlers.

BUCKS BED ABOVE AND DOWNWIND OF THEIR BACKTRAIL

Mature bucks have been followed by coyotes, lions, and people since they were fawns. By maturity, they've learned to bed downwind of their backtrail to catch the scent of any following predator. In steep terrain, bucks often bed where they can see their backtrail, usually on the uphill side, fortifying their defenses. You must stay downwind and uphill of a track to have any chance at a shot.

In many tracking jobs, fast judging and shooting skills are required. Some trophy hunters don't like tracking, as it's difficult to identify antlers quickly (not all big-bodied deer have big antlers) and they have thus accidentally shot smaller-antlered bucks. They've got a point, but I believe knowing how to track will hang more big bucks than ignoring the technique. Quick-shooting, jam-free rifles are a must, and you have to keep your scope on 4x or less.

Neither this book nor even fifty books could teach you everything about tracking, but here are some suggestions to improve your tracking game.

START TRACKING DEER

There is no season on tracking. Much of what I've learned has come from just tracking deer, any deer, and paying attention to how they use the terrain. You will be amazed at how much you'll learn about bucks by just tracking them. They will show you where they bed, where they feed, where they never go, and what times of the day they go where. You'll also learn which conditions are good for tracking. When snow is crunchy and frozen or the bare earth is frozen or just won't take and hold a track, you might have to choose another technique, but you'll still need to be aware of the tracks in the area. Deer are telling you where they are and what they are doing by their tracks, so don't ignore them.

When tracking, many hunters falsely assume
they'll catch the buck in the open

More often than not you're only going to get a quick or partial
glimpse of the buck. Fast accurate shooting is almost always required.

READ

The Benoit Brothers are the best whitetail trackers in the country. Deer are deer, though, and much of what the Benoits teach applies to tracking mule deer. There are two excellent books that are a must-read for anyone wanting to pick up the track of a good buck: *Big Bucks the Benoit Way* and *Benoit Bucks*, both by Bryce Towsley. Much of the country they track in is gentler than the West, but you'll still learn a lot by following them on the hunt for huge whitetails in the thick and nasty.

Another excellent read is Tom Brown Jr.'s *The Science and Art of Tracking*. Tom was trained by one of the last Apache trackers. He teaches that tracking is just an awareness of one's surroundings, and he's right. Trackers are separated by their skills, and their skills are separated by their awareness, pure and simple. While he gets deep into the metaphysical aspects of tracking, I find his physical description of tracking the most in-depth available anywhere. All my tracking added up is but a grain of sand compared with his experience.

Tracking is primal and satisfies something deep in a hunter's soul. It's been practiced for thousands of years on every continent. I think if you don't learn to track, you're not only missing out on the fun, you also won't be nearly as successful. While you likely won't take a lot of your big mule deer by only tracking, I think you'll find as you kill a few big mule deer that tracking and awareness of tracks will have played a big part in that success.

I learned from Tom Brown Jr.'s books and experience to always put the track between yourself and the sun. Here, these tracks are invisible because the sun is behind me

Here I've put the same tracks between myself and
the sun – and they stand out like beacons!

DEER DRIVES

N O MULE DEER BOOK WOULD BE COMPLETE without the mention of deer drives. They've been used for thousands of years to put game in front of hunters, and even today many hunters are successful using deer drives. In my younger years, my family frequently did deer drives and sometimes they even worked. However, I don't use them much anymore for a few reasons.

Most men, me included, take the bulldozer approach to life, i.e. we plow through everything like a D9 CAT in an effort to reach our goals. If something isn't working, we look for a bigger hammer. Big mature mule deer, though, do not operate that way. They are slow and methodical and think about their every move.

By nature, a deer drive is forcing a buck to do what he doesn't want to do, and the outcome is unpredictable. Big bucks rarely paint themselves into a corner, and they nearly always will have multiple escape routes at their disposal. Add in the fact that they don't often pause once the manure hits the propeller, and the chances of getting off an accurate shot drop precipitously.

Walking with my son Cash – future deer hunting partner?

I've learned that killing mature bucks requires finesse; the path of the quiet and stealthy is the best for me. Moving at a buck's speed and letting him make the decisions usually makes for a more predictable outcome. I want to take a buck more or less on his own terms.

But to say I won't ever use deer drives for big mule deer would be foolish. I'm an outfitter and often have clients who insist on trying a deer drive. While it rarely works, sometimes late in the hunt it's worth a try and I succumb to their pleading. Also, not everyone is patient enough to work the other tactics when the chips are down. A deer drive at least "feels like" you're doing something. As I look into my young son's eyes and see the hunter brewing inside, I can envision the day when he finally gets to sit the knob while his old man beats the brush hoping some horny-headed buck makes his escape in front of my son's surely wavering deer rifle. When those days come, I'll remember a few things about deer drives that I've learned over the years.

IT TAKES AN UNSELFISH BUNCH

I had the good fortune of hunting with some of the best hunters I know who use deer drives to kill big mule deer. Brian Suter of Thayne, Wyoming, along with his family were noted in the 1980s and '90s as the deer-drive connoisseurs. One year in the early '90s while hunting the Hoback country of western Wyoming, I sat on a knob glassing some pristine beautiful high country when below me, none other than Brian himself walked out of the timber. I immediately recognized him from some videos I'd watched. We talked a few minutes and true to the nature of many backcountry deer hunters, he invited me to hunt with him, his brother Dennis, and a nephew whose name has long escaped me. Within a few days, I was initiated to the high-country deer drive. While I never killed a buck on that hunt, I learned quickly why after opening day there are no big bucks roaming the picturesque basins – they're hiding in the trees! I saw multiple bucks those days that I wouldn't have seen any other way other than forcing them to move.

Deer drives aren't complicated. The Suters would pick a manageable-sized piece of cover adjacent to known feed areas, post a shooter or two along suspected escape routes where visibility was good, and then have several hunters slowly work the cover. They – true to form of big buck hunters – didn't make a bunch of noise in an effort to move deer. Rather, they just hunted slowly through the cover knowing that big bucks hear everything and would likely move. They never felt like the posted shooters were the only ones who were going to get the shooting, as they hunted slowly and quietly enough that they could realistically get a shot at a bruiser as he made his escape (if I remember right, Brian killed his incredible 244-7/8" non-typical buck as a driver.) As they moved through the timber and brush, they would keep the other drivers in sight as much as possible, not just for safety, but also to keep bucks from slipping back between them. Sometimes they kept the wind in their favor; other times they let it take their scent to likely areas. At the end of a drive, they would move to another piece of cover and do it all over again. They were unselfish and worked together for the good of the bunch. If someone would kill a great buck, they all took pride in the accomplishment, as they should.

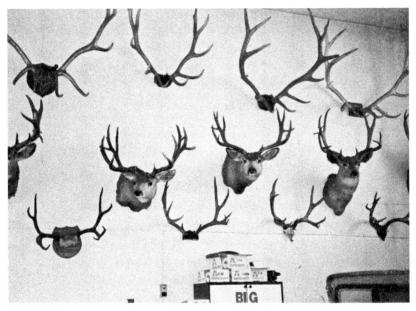

The Suter brothers took these big bucks and many more using deer drives.

Later that season, Brian invited me to stop by his mechanic shop located along Wyoming's Salt River. It was filled with great mounts of many bucks between 180" and 200" and a few bigger, including Brian's incredible non-typical spreading over 40 inches. Many of the bucks had been taken on deer drives, attesting to their effectiveness. I decided then and there that if you could assemble a team of hunters who were unselfish enough to hunt for the good of the group, they could kill some great bucks. Even though I've never found that group and usually hunt alone, you'll never hear me relegate a deer drive to the ineffective column.

Just remember, shots are quick, wounding loss is higher, and you don't always get to pick your buck. Deer drives can be employed from high country to desert as long as there is enough cover to hide a buck. In almost all deer country, there are trails leading in and out of the cover. If at all possible, try to cover those trails. If you're a driver, hunt quietly, keep your partners in sight, your eyes peeled, and your rifle ready. If you're a poster, don't space out at the birds circling above or at the moose grazing below. Keep still and quiet, listening for any movement – usually the first clue that bucks are on the move – and keep your rifle in your hands. Know all the yardages you might be shooting to from your sniper perch. Make sure you're practiced at shooting at moving animals and keep plenty of ammo in reach. Everyone should wear blaze orange and practice the utmost in safety. Radios are helpful at the end of a drive to regroup and plan, but they're too noisy to have on during the drive unless you don't care about getting a shot off.

Few things in big buck hunting are as exciting as knowing bucks are on the move and could appear in range at any second. You will feel as alive as you've ever been when the branches start cracking and the rifles begin to roar.

LONG-RANGE HUNTING

I CAN'T THINK OF A SUBJECT THAT HAS STIRRED MORE controversy in the hunting world than the long-range craze of the last ten years. The rise of the long-range hunter is evident everywhere: shooting schools teaching long-range proficiency beyond 1,000 yards, TV shows featuring long-range hunting, and specialty long-range rifles and equipment becoming mainstream.

You should have noticed by now that this book isn't very political. I haven't offered my thoughts or proposed solutions on big game management, growing trophy bucks, predator control, public lands, landowner tags, and the many other political subjects that hunters entangle themselves within. It's not that I'm not a political person. If you knew me, you'd agree that I am. However, this book is about becoming a great mule deer hunter.

So also on the subject of long-range hunting, I'm going to leave the politics out. The fight over long-range hunting is just beginning and I don't know where it will end. I do know that no matter what our states decide, I'll still be out in the deer woods with whatever weapon is legal and probably killing some big mule deer. So will you if you want to. My intent is to offer opinion on the need for long-range ability for the big mule deer hunter.

Hunters sometimes ask me if it's necessary to shoot long range to kill big mule deer. That's a great question because if the ability to shoot long range is necessary, then it could also be called a technique, just like glassing, still-hunting, or tracking. However, to answer that question, I need to have a definition of long-range hunting. That can be problematic, because "long range" is a relative term. What is long range for one hunter might not be for another. It depends on your personal skill level. Some hunters wound more game at 200 yards than others wound at 700.

Based on my own experience, here is *my* definition of long-range hunting:

Intending to shoot a buck at at least double your maximum effective range.

For my definition, you have to know your maximum effective range in real hunting conditions – not just target conditions – as this will take in how you personally handle yourself when the pressure is on. You can do that only by running the math on all your shots at big game, and I think you need to have a sample size of at least 10 shots. If you don't, you should stick to shots under 300 yards anyway and skip to the next chapter.

I've killed over 90 percent of the bucks I've aimed at out to 300 yards; 100 percent is unattainable in real hunting conditions. If I now *intend* to kill bucks beyond 600 yards, I've entered the "Robby" definition of long range. This definition can apply to archery and muzzleloader hunting, too, although a factor of 1.5x rather than 2x is probably more applicable.

With that definition and my personal stats taken into account, there have been zero – yes zero – times in my 35+ years of hunting where I've needed to shoot 600 yards to kill a big buck. I've always been able to get closer, which truly is the exciting hunting part. Based on my definition, I don't think you need to be a long-range hunter to kill big mule deer. However, I still call it a technique, as those who intend to kill a buck at long range are using it as a technique. I'll let the mobs argue the ethics of it all.

Just last fall on an Idaho hunt, I killed an 8-year-old buck when I could not get any closer than 420 yards. When I spotted him I was beyond 600 yards, but I cut the distance to 420, greatly improving the chance of a kill shot. I was shooting an extremely accurate Cooper Excalibur Model 52 in 7mm Remington Magnum that regularly recorded ½ MOA 3-shot groups; I had practiced with it out to 600 yards. But getting closer improved my chances of a clean kill – and our quarry deserves that – so I did. I would have gotten even closer if I could have.

Personally, I think a hunter needs to be able to shoot out to 600 yards with a rifle, 150 with a muzzleloader, and 70 with a bow. A friend of mine who used to guide in Oregon told me that they restricted their bowhunters during archery season to 50-yard shots, and the guiding contract specified that any hunter trying a longer shot would be sent home with no refund. There never was any argument, till one year a young and very savvy hunter showed up and requested an exception. He said he'd practiced all year on 70- or 75-yard shots and was quite accurate at that distance. The guides put a paper plate on a straw bale and walked off 75 yards, and the kid put 10 out of 10 arrows in the pie plate. He got the exception.

I think hunters should restrict themselves to the ranges noted above, BUT a hunter should always intend to get as close as possible. I don't go to the deer woods with the intent of hunting long range, but I make sure I'm ready to shoot to those listed yardages if need be. Based on my career hunting statistics, so should you.

GLASSING

I believe glassing is a big buck hunter's number one technique. The term glassing to me means using various optics at all yardages from short to extreme to find deer you can't readily see with the naked eye. Its purposes are for finding a particular buck or bucks and for planning how to make the kill.

By glassing, I don't just mean spot-and-stalk hunting, which really is a sub-technique to glassing. Spot-and-stalk to me is shooting a buck you've stalked within a few hours after spotting him. Glassing is using optics to simply find deer and plan your hunt. The kill could happen seconds, minutes, days, or even weeks later by any technique – spot-and-stalk, tracking, ambush hunting – but would have never happened without glassing.

I've found that unless I'm handy with the other techniques I've laid out in this book, glassing alone won't get it done, and that's why I saved it for last. Virtually every one of the big deer I've taken was killed by some combination of these techniques. I might glass up a great deer, but if he disappears into the cover, it's going to be tracking, still-hunting, obeying the wind, and ambush hunting that will get me the shot. But it all starts with glassing.

Most articles on mule deer focus so heavily on the use of optics that a hunter begins to think that is all there is to mule deer hunting. As I've written throughout this book, hunted mule deer live close to the cover – and while optics play a super important role in finding deer, you can't just glass and kill big bucks, at least not very many. I'll give you some examples of what I mean.

To make ends meet at home, I've been an outfitter for going on 15 seasons. I operate exclusively on managed private land that I know very well. By the first of September I've usually seen most of the big bucks on the properties I manage through my summer scouting. During the summer, I rarely have to do anything but glass key areas to find them. However, once they lose their velvet and hunting season approaches, they become very difficult to find. I don't host archery deer hunts, so there is no hunting pressure on these bucks before October. They just naturally move into the cover.

By the time my rifle hunters arrive in early October, big buck sightings are down at least 50 percent. My guides and I still start most days with glassing just like I do in July, but we focus on the heaviest cover. We still spot our bucks, but killing them isn't just setting down the optics and pulling the trigger or starting the stalk. We have to employ every technique in this book to kill them. In 15 years, I can think of only one big buck we actually spotted and stalked and killed in the classic manner that so many articles have detailed. All the rest of the big bucks have come by a combination of still-hunting, moving carefully, obeying the wind, tracking, and ambush hunting, like the following story illustrates – and keep in mind that if what I'm about to tell you applies on lightly hunted private land, it über-applies to hunting on public land.

DARYL MUÑOZ

Ol' Daryl Muñoz was one of my first clients in my scouting business and later took interest in hunting the ranches I manage for bucks and bulls. In his late 60s and self-admittedly "long in the tooth," Daryl has to take the slow approach to big buck hunting.

He often jokes that if he starts walking before first light, he'll be out the camper door by sunrise.

While guiding Daryl on the ranch, even if I spotted a 180" buck at two miles, bedded him under a serviceberry bush, got the wind in our favor, then started the

stalk, chances are low we'd kill that buck.

In that brushy country (which mirrors most of the brushy country in the West where I've seen giant mule deer), the buck would likely be very hard to find once we got within range, either because he'd moved or because the topography just wouldn't allow you to see into his bed.

Last fall, Daryl arrived on October 8. I'd thoroughly scouted the ranch he was hunting and had located about four bucks between 170" and 190" that Daryl would certainly be happy with. Because they'd rubbed their velvet, I'd only caught glimpses of them in the last few weeks; they'd moved into areas with more brush and timber.

The guides arrived on the eve of the opener and I showed them every place we needed to have eyes on over the next five days. Matt Capson and Tyler Williams have guided for me for years and know the ranches well. I had another hunter in camp, too, so there would be three guides to two hunters.

Come sunrise the next day, the guides and I were in key positions looking through a combined total of optics of around $15,000 (we all use Swarovski binoculars and spotting scopes). Daryl was stalking the cover alone but waiting for our call (radios are legal in Idaho while hunting) if he needed to be somewhere else. My other hunter stuck close to us, as he wasn't as familiar with the ranch.

I would love to say that by 10:00 a.m. we had two big bucks bedded and waiting for our hunters to start the stalk, but I know that isn't how it usually rolls with big deer in the West, so I wasn't disappointed. Rather, it was the typical hunt where at least one of us had spotted a good buck but just couldn't keep track of him before he made the cover. Undaunted, we spent the next five days repeating this routine. On day four, my other hunter – who was a joy to have in camp but had grown tired of seeing big bucks escape before we made it in range – told me, "Rob, I like your operation and have had a great time, but the next buck of any legal size that makes a mistake is

going to hear from my 7-mag."

Just a few hours later, the guides and I helped him get his 3x4 buck off the mountain and into the truck. He'd killed it by still-hunting through the cover where we'd seen some good bucks in the previous days. He said that just as the evening sun set, he jumped two deer from their beds at less than 80 yards. One of them was one of the big bucks we'd been trying to get the drop on, but he couldn't get a shot. The younger less experienced buck wasn't so quick and my hunter made a great shot.

The next day was the last day. At our nightly pow-wow, we all agreed that Daryl should set an ambush in an area where we'd seen our second-best buck appear a few times during the week. He was visible only when the sun was below either horizon, and there was never enough time to make a stalk – that buck was no dummy. Daryl, always patient and never in a hurry, readily agreed. Tyler had to return to work, and I could guide only for the morning as I had to meet my incoming elk hunters. I put Matt in charge and they decided that he and I would stay back about 1,000 yards where we could glass all of the brushy hillside where the buck had showed himself while Daryl set an ambush point that would put him within 300 yards.

The next morning Matt and I were on the glass watching the hillside. I spotted the good buck just as the sun was cresting the eastern horizon behind me. He was within 150 yards of Daryl's position, feeding at a good pace toward an aspen stand that would soon swallow him up like a marble dropped in the ocean. We radioed Daryl, who couldn't reply because he'd spook the buck, and we gave him the general directions to the buck. We never heard his ol' aught-six go off before the buck vanished into the trees.

Back at camp, Daryl said he could see two deer where we'd indicated, but the brush was too thick to tell which one was a good buck (we'd seen only one buck, attesting to the thickness of the cover). That's normal for a big buck to show himself only where just parts of him can be seen. As I departed for town, I shook Daryl's hand and wished him luck for the last evening hunt.

By dark I'd met my elk hunters and escorted them to their camp on another part of the ranch where they'd start hunting the next day. I had to be back to their camp before sunrise to guide them, so I was anxious to get home and sleep in a real bed before I started another seven days of guiding. This ranch is about 20 miles from my home, so I hit the gravel road that led to momma. Just as the small city lights of my hometown began to shine in the distance, my cell phone came to life. It was Matt.

"I think Daryl got him! Come up and help me!"

I jammed on the brakes and flipped my old Ford around and headed for their camp – so much for a good night's rest! Pulling into camp, I found the place was alive. Daryl and Matt were retelling the story and had even got the ranch hand involved in the excitement. Tyler, back at home, kept ringing Matt's phone hoping to get in on the action. It's funny how hunters come back to life when a big buck hits the dirt.

Soon Matt and I were headed back up the mountain in the dark to get the buck. As we fought the brush, he recounted the story. Matt said they were both in position by 4:30 p.m. and for nearly three boring hours, there was zero action. By the last few minutes of light, Matt had glassed only a few does. It was too dark to see the hillside anymore, nearly 1,000 yards distant, so he packed up his optics and headed for the truck a short distance away.

KaaPOWwwwwwwwwwwwwwwwwwwwww

"What the?" Matt thought. He held his radio to his ear and listened intently, knowing not to bother a man on a rifle. A few minutes later ol' Daryl lit up the radio with an enthusiastic "Hear that?!"

Matt shot back, "What happened?"

Daryl explained that just as it was almost too dark to see, he spotted the buck standing at the edge of the aspen patch checking to see if the coast was clear before he fed into the open. The range was almost 300 yards and the buck was facing him, but Daryl couldn't wait even a few moments or he wouldn't be able to see. Daryl is a superb shot (he's fired three shots on my ranches over the years and killed three animals), and he promptly put the buck on his nose. Reports like that make an outfitter smile.

As we reached the buck's side, I could indeed see it was that second-best buck we'd been hunting. He was long and heavy and would score well into the 170" range, even without eyeguards. I could tell by his body size that he was an older deer. Rolling him over, we found Daryl's bullet hole just at the base of

233

the neck. Daryl had hit a pie plate-sized target in near darkness at 300 yards with only a few seconds to prepare for the shot. There's something to be said about slow old men who've been shooting 30.06s since they were kids.

Daryl's ambush had worked and I believe it was the only way we could have killed that buck.

However, it all started with glassing. Had we not known where this buck was, which we figured out by extensive glassing, we could have set a thousand ambushes and never killed him.

A big mule deer hunter must know how to glass if he's going to tie his tag on a big buck.

Another view of Daryl's buck.

234

GLASSING TECHNIQUE

Knowing how to glass is even more important than the optics themselves. Let's consider how to use binoculars and spotting scopes. I could be a poseur and lay out the system I use as if it were my own, but that would not only be unethical, it would also rob you of a chance to learn from one of the best DIY hunters out there, David Long.

In David's excellent 2006 book *Public Land Mule Deer, The Bottom Line*, he explains his four-phase glassing system. While any great mule deer hunter, given enough years, would probably arrive at the same system David uses, to my knowledge he was the first to put the system to paper – and he did it thoughtfully and effectively.

Basically, in four-phase glassing, you move from the first phase – looking with your binoculars at all of the terrain in sight – then progressing in detail and intensity through the remaining phases until you're picking every bush, tree, and shrub apart with your spotting scope in the last phase. For a complete explanation, I highly recommend his book. The only thing I'd add to David's method is a pre-phase of looking at everything within long rifle range with your naked eye. The human eye is underestimated, in my opinion, and I've spotted several of my best bucks with the naked eye, even out to one mile.

Before you employ David's system, you must be proficient at actually "seeing" what is in your optics, whether you're using binoculars or a spotting scope. Learning how to glass takes some time, as you have to train the brain

235

and the eyes to work together in a way they naturally don't. It starts with steadying your optics, dividing up your field of view into a grid, then spending time looking at each section of the grid.

Deer, undisturbed, move about every three to five seconds unless they're sleeping. That means you have to look at each section of the grid at least that long; it's often movement that will get your attention first. If the deer isn't hidden, you'll likely see him quickly, but if you don't slow down and study, you'll miss more deer than you see.

Big bucks move slowly and stay close to cover, making them hard to spot.

In a season or two, your eyes and brain will start to "see" in a way that makes glassing effective.

I think glassing is most like putting together a 1,000-piece jigsaw puzzle of a mountain. You have to study each piece to eventually put the puzzle together successfully. Once you're done, you know every detail on the mountain – like certain trees, rocks, and other features that weren't noticeable when you first looked at the picture of the mountain on the puzzle box. Before you put the puzzle together, you had only "the big picture" of the mountain and didn't notice the small features. When I'm with an inexperienced glasser, that is what I find he is doing. He can see the mountain, but he's not studying the small features – and it's why steady optics are important, so you can see the small stuff.

I've had the rare opportunity to hunt with two different hunters who had each lost an eye. In both cases, I was the first to introduce them to big buck hunting. I thought I'd really have to help them see deer – after all, how well could a guy see with one eye? Yet I found that both men had excellent vision when it came to seeing deer. In the days we hunted together, both of them showed me several bucks I'd missed spotting. Also, one of my guides in my outfitting business, Tyler Williams, has a genetic eye disease and yet is one of the best glassers I've ever hunted with.

For years since their handicap, all these hunters have honed their brains' ability to "see" what is coming through their eyes. In the deer woods, spotting a gray animal in a gray environment, an animal that often moves very slowly or not at all isn't hard for them. I can't explain how they all are able to do this, but I guess it's because they've learned to focus their brains on what they are looking at, whereas all of us 20/20 two-eyed guys have never had a reason to do that. Our eyes "wander" across the scene in front of us; we don't naturally notice details. Even if I can't easily explain it, hunting with these guys proves to me that you can train your brain to "see" what your eyes are looking at.

My friend Eddie Irigoyen. Note his binoculars have only one barrel! He's trained his brain to see bucks as well as anyone.

Tyler Williams has a genetic eye disease but behind the glass, he is one of the best I've seen.

My friend Doug Swanson, who also lost an eye, is excellent at spotting bucks.

The best way to do this is to glass a lot through steady optics. I never go near deer country without optics, giving me ample practice to train my brain and eyes to work together. I'd estimate I spend at least 100 hours per year behind optics but to be honest, other than the fact I'm more patient and I hunt better now, I don't think I'm much better at glassing than I was 20 years ago. My point is that you can become rather proficient in just a few years. In a season or two, your eyes and brain will start to work together in a way that makes glassing most effective. After that, the law of diminishing returns seems to take over; you'll get better, until your eyes begin to seriously age, but at much smaller increments.

SPOT-AND-STALK HUNTING

In pure spot-and-stalk hunting, you're using your optics to find undisturbed bucks. Once located, you plan your approach to get within range to make a killing shot, usually within a few hours after spotting the buck.

This is the technique most hunters attempt to use. However, in most hunted populations of mule deer, you can't just spot and stalk. Big bucks might hang out in the open for only a few minutes each day if there's even a hint of hunting pressure. However, spot-and-stalk is still a viable technique.

In this day and age, I think spot-and-stalk is best used in the early August and September seasons, but there has to be little hunting pressure for it to work. This could be an archery, muzzleloader, or rifle hunt, as long as there are few hunters afield and the bucks are still using the open country. Of course I've spotted and stalked bucks all fall into the early winter seasons, but it's most effective in the early season, especially if the bucks are still in velvet. I've killed three big mule deer with a bow in the early seasons. All these bucks were taken the first week of September and all of them relied heavily on spot-and-stalk.

239

I spotted this public-land buck in late morning and spent four hours closing
the distance to 40 yards. He eventually stood, giving me a killing shot.

Another public-land buck I spotted and stalked. I found him at
daylight after a big storm. I was able to close the distance
and ambush him as he headed for cover.

I've killed bucks later in the fall using spot-and-stalk, but not very many as it's so hard to keep track of them before they head for the trees.

I killed this buck on the last day of the Idaho general season in 2012 with spot-and-stalk. I'd spotted him bedded at daylight and closed the distance to 200 yards. A few hours later he stood up to feed and I made the shot.

THE BROKEN HEART BUCK

Here's another story to illustrate how spot-and-stalk usually works out.

There is a low brushy ridge on the east side of one of the ranches I manage in southeast Idaho. It's nothing remarkable, just a ridge. It runs less than a mile separating some hayfields to the east from a sea of aspen and sage to the west. When the September rut starts, it's a magnet for bull elk that gather cows from the fields below and push them into the ridge's thick cover. Once in a while I've even seen a nice buck there, but nothing too special. That all changed early one August morning.

Out on a sagebrush knob rising from the ridge stood a great buck. He saw me first and like a good running back, bounded over and around the sagebrush before making the cover. Even with my naked eye, I could see he had great height, good mass, and some extra points. He was nearly 30 inches wide. Excited, I made plans to hunt him when archery season opened.

As summer gave way to fall, I hunted the buck almost daily. By late September, I'd put in 20 days without even a glimpse of him. The aspen jungles seemed to have swallowed him up. My archery elk hunters were due in a few days and I hoped to find him before they stirred the place up.

On a clear, cold morning, walking under a canvas of stars, my thoughts wandered back over the days since our first encounter and I had to remind myself that I really had seen a giant buck. I set up a half-mile from the brushy

242

ridge in the early dawn, and waited for light. Stars disappeared one by one and a cold breeze picked up, stinging my face and hands.

I pulled my old seven-power binoculars from my fleece jacket and began glassing the emerging landscape. Just before sunrise, a lone buck stood from his bed in the open sage. There was no question it was him. He had 6-inch bases and at least 20-inch G-2's. I was a little disappointed to see he was missing his right G-4, but on a buck like this one, score is not everything. With an enormous body, and antlers pushing 30 inches wide, he was certainly a sight to behold.

He worked his way out of the sagebrush into the cover without a ray of sunshine touching him. The bow lying at my feet seemed like a child's toy. In weeks of searching the aspen stands, I'd managed to see him only two times. How would I ever get an arrow in a buck that was rarely out of the cover?

The aspen and sage country the big buck called home.
Some of those quakie pockets are thick enough to hide a bulldozer.

After spending a few days with my elk hunters, I left them with the other guides and started after the buck one morning at dawn. I studied every deer track I could find, but none seemed to be from a big-bodied buck. I hunted him daily until archery season closed, without another sighting.

The October rifle deer hunt opened five days before the elk hunt, and I glassed and stalked the cover for those five days, too. He just seemed to have evaporated. Once elk season opened, I was busy for a week helping my hunters. Several had deer tags and hunted the brush-choked area, but by the time elk season closed, no one had spotted hide nor hair of him. I resumed hunting him the next morning but over the next six days, saw only a few bucks.

As the night turned to day on October 28, I glassed a knob west of the brushy ridge. The leaves had fallen and the ranch was taking on the gray hues of winter. It reminded me of hunting other southeast Idaho brush country with my father nearly 30 years ago. Within minutes, I spotted a group of does about 1,000 yards out at the edge of an aspen thicket. A big-bodied deer stood amongst them. I ripped my pack from my shoulder and quickly set up my 30x Swarovski. It was him!

He was in full rut, following each doe until she'd stop and let him check her. The morning sun illuminated his rack in a way I hadn't seen it before. Again, he was a sight to behold. This was likely the only chance I'd have. I headed into the cover straight for him, ducking under branches as I tried to keep my Weatherby slung over my shoulder.

I emerged slowly from the aspen and spotted the does across a 200-yard sagebrush flat. I dropped to my rear and steadied my rifle. The does were alert, but he wasn't visible. After a few minutes, they nervously made their way into the aspen. I made a circle to the north and spotted him walking at 250 yards just at the brush's edge. I hit the ground and brought the rifle up, but he made the cover before I could shoot. A dreadful feeling crept over me. Over the next hour of watching and waiting, it became clear that he'd given me the slip. My heart felt like it was breaking.

I hunted every day until the last evening, when in the fading light of Halloween, I shot a narrow 7x7 buck for the freezer. I called Dad for help and sat down by the dead deer to watch the stars come out. I'd put in over 40 days on one buck, yet had managed to see him only three times. I felt crushed to have lost the only opportunity I had, but thanked God for a great season.

Soon I could see the headlights of Dad's truck bouncing up the dirt road below. I stood and shined my flashlight his way. Upon arriving, he was excited about the nice buck lying at my feet, and my spirits lifted a little.

It was a long winter hoping and praying the big buck would make it back to the ranch. Come July, I started scouting but found only elk and average bucks. Then one early August morning, I was walking an old two-track at first light when I spotted some deer on the same sagebrush knob where I'd first seen him. I set up my 500mm Canon lens and camera and hunkered down.

One buck looked very tall with a huge body. I studied his velvet-donned antlers carefully in the spawning light. He was heavy but didn't have cheaters like the buck from the previous season, nor did he seem as wide. He did, however, have an inline point on his right G-3 exactly like what I'd seen the year before. I snapped a few photos as he moved away.

Back at home, I enlarged the photos and could see it was indeed him, but he'd regressed some. His former cheaters were now just bumps and his G-4 had only grown several inches off the beam. He was still a great deer; he just didn't have as much bone as the year before. I was thankful for another chance at him and prepared for the archery hunt.

I hunted the first week without seeing him. On September 5, I was up at 4:30 yet again. Although tired, I faithfully walked the dirt road toward his brushy hideout in the predawn darkness as a cold breeze nipped at my exposed skin. I arrived at my glassing point by first light and sat down. Pulling the collar of my wool shirt close to my neck, I glassed the same knob where I'd seen him with the does the previous October. It wasn't long before I spotted three bucks feeding a few yards out of the cover. The huge body gave him away. His velvet-tan rack bobbed several feet over his head as he fed along, making the other nice bucks look like youngsters. I was hoping he'd bed in the open where I could plan a stalk.

I called my wife and she got the kids together by the phone to pray for Daddy. They all wanted me to finally close the deal, but I prayed with my eyes open, afraid he'd disappear if I looked away. The bucks soon fed back into the brush without bedding. My only chance was to creep through the cover with the wind in my face. I might not get a shot, but this buck was so elusive, I took a gamble and went for it.

Once in the cover, I nocked an arrow and slowed way down, moving about 100 yards over the next 30 minutes. I carefully and quietly placed each step as I picked the brush apart with my eyes. The hillside was covered with volcanic cinder, making it hard to be silent. My focus wandered between being quiet and trying to see through the tangle. There was no margin for error.

Suddenly, I heard deer get up in front of me. Straining to see through a big serviceberry bush, I spotted two deer sneaking away. I slowly sank to my knees and peered around the bush as they stopped and looked nervously back. He was the lead buck. I quickly ranged him at 63 yards.

I pulled my Martin Phantom. Through my peep, he looked to be quartering away at a fair angle, so I put my 60-yard pin high on his last rib and released. He bunched up and leaped 15 feet, then bolted around the knob. A bewildered 3-point followed suit.

I thought I'd missed, but couldn't find the arrow after an hour's search. Getting down on hands and knees, I crawled along the buck's escape route looking for any sign of a hit. I was surprised to find that he did not have a large track. He was like a 250-pound guy with a size 7 boot. That explained why I was never able to identify his track the last two years.

One hundred yards later, I found blood. I became excited and worried all at once. Spattered at first, it then picked up to a palm-sized puddle every 50 yards or so. My gut tied itself in a knot as I carefully picked the buck's tracks from the other deer, cattle, and elk tracks strewn about. It would take me 10 minutes to find the next track, then 10 more to confirm it was his. I badly wanted to see him piled up in the sage and end the tension. My knees were getting sore and my light wool gloves hung in tatters.

Seven hours and 400 yards later, I lost all sign in the tall grass of an aspen stand. I sat on the ground and pulled my sore knees to my chest. My heart felt heavy and broken. I couldn't comprehend losing this deer after working so hard for him for so long. With tears in my eyes, I cursed myself for taking a risky shot. I prayed for God's help. Walking back to the truck as evening approached, thoughts crashed through my head.

"Maybe he wasn't quartering away as much as I thought and I held too far back?"

"Maybe I just nicked him and he'd be fine to hunt another day?"

These thoughts haunted me for three weeks as I searched for him almost daily. In that time, I found other bucks I'd seen him with, but I never saw him. He was such an elusive deer, I held hope he was alive and well.

In the last few days of the season I found the fallen giant in a thick aspen patch. The birds and coyotes had done their job, even stripping the velvet from his antlers.

It was heartbreakingly sad to see him in such a condition. A few feet from his barren ribcage lay the arrow. He died within an hour of my shot and only made it about 700 yards. In that brushy country, that isn't much different than twenty miles.

He'd broken my heart many times, but in the end I'd broken his. I twisted his skull from his bleached spine and started the long hike back for the truck.

I've had a few seasons to think and pray about it, and as memories often do, they've grown sweeter with time. While it didn't end the way I'd hoped, I had finally connected with the one buck that had captured my heart and mind for so long. And for that, Dear God, I am thankful.

I had finally connected on the buck that had held my attention for two long seasons.

247

I'll never forget the days and weeks I spent looking for him. In two years I saw him only a few times, but the hunt will forever be etched in my mind.

That story should illustrate my point again that spot-and-stalk as a technique is rarely useful without other techniques. In the case of this buck, I had to consider the wind, move very carefully, and rely on a dose of still-hunting to get the shot. That launches us into another sub-technique of glassing.

EXTREME LONG-RANGE GLASSING

Back in the late 1990s I was a scouting fool. I'd spend nearly as much time in the summer looking for bucks as I did hunting them in the fall. I was putting 300 miles a year on a saddlehorse. I learned a ton of country and it's one reason for my success. I also learned the value of extreme long-range glassing – distances beyond two miles – in that time.

I remember scouting one Idaho unit that held relatively few deer. Because it wasn't very good hunting, most hunters either didn't go there or gave up after a day or two of no buck sightings. It was indeed a frustrating place to hunt, but looking at some of the bucks on the winter range from that unit proved to me that there was a whopper or two or three to be had.

One cold October evening I sat on a ridge as the sun began to set behind me, illuminating the landscape to the east. When the sun is rising or setting, the rays of light travel almost parallel to the land, improving your ability to spot bucks like no other time of day. I'd been hunting four or five days and had hardly seen any bucks. I could see a "bucky" peak over four miles east of my position that had a skiff of October snow. The sun would soon be down, so I set up my spotter hoping to catch a buck contrasted against the background of snow on the peak. At the time, I was using a 20x compact Leupold spotter and Leupold tripod. While the effort to spot a buck at that distance seemed futile, I gave it a shot. About 15 minutes into my glassing session, with the sun illuminating the slopes of the peak, I saw a really nice buck walk between two timber patches. At that distance, all I could see was that he had antlers that were about the same height as the distance between his brisket and top of his shoulders – roughly 20 inches – indicating a pretty good buck. I had to leave the next day and wouldn't be able to return before the season closed, so I didn't get to hunt that buck. However, I vowed to return to scout that country the following summer.

The following August, I made a very long horseback ride into that country. I started scouting on the same ridge where I'd seen that good buck the previous October. Within a few days I'd seen several really good bucks, including one of the few Boone and Crockett net typicals I've ever seen. I've killed several big mule deer there and have seen many more good bucks there over the years. Had I not been using a spotter and using it correctly, I may have never found that place, especially since most of the unit held very few good bucks. I'd have given up and searched for greener pastures.

It makes no sense to pack a spotter or high-power binocular and look only at the country you can hunt that same day. Look instead at everything within rifle range and out to five miles if the conditions are right. If you plan your hunt or scout right, you can find places where you can be looking at more than several bucky areas even miles apart in one glassing session. When you start glassing like this, your odds of finding a big buck will skyrocket.

With the rising sun at my back, I glass a mountain three miles distant through 15x56 Vortex tripod mounted binoculars.

The view from three miles. With practice, you can
spot bucks at these distances and even farther.

You may have noticed that I have killed several of my best bucks days after I spotted them from extreme ranges. That is why I know the technique works. Before you try it, you may have to get over a few preconceived notions. First, you're not going to be scoring bucks at these ranges. With practice, though, you'll learn to identify big bucks by other factors besides just antlers – including body size and behavior. It's more of an art than it is a science, but you can become proficient at it.

Second, you have to "believe" that mule deer bucks really don't wander far. If you don't, you'll convince yourself that any buck you spot from extreme distance will be long gone by the time you get there. Third, like tracking, you can't glass extreme distances every day. The conditions have to be right for it to work. You need to have the sun at your back with no cloud cover at the prime hours when bucks are moving. Snow makes for a great background as long as there's no fog and there's also enough light available to see long distance. Finally, extreme glassing isn't just for the backcountry. Many hunters would be shocked to know how many big deer I've spotted from major highways *and even from within city limits* as I've glassed country under ideal conditions from three, four, and even five miles away.

The value of extreme long range glassing is like that of aerial scouting. It's not just about finding a particular buck, but finding country that bucks call home and then planning your hunt accordingly.

THE COMPLETE MULE DEER HUNTER

S O THERE YOU HAVE THE NINE TECHNIQUES YOU NEED for killing big mule deer everywhere they live. You now have everything you need – minus practice – to kill the best buck of your life. Remember, though, that for the complete deer hunter, the techniques don't function exclusively. Rather, each technique has overlap with other techniques: glassing might show you a big buck that can be killed only by ambush; while setting an ambush, you might discover a smoking hot big blocky track and have to switch to tracking right then. Then while tracking that big buck through a series of broken draws, you lose his track but know he isn't far, so you still-hunt for a few hours in the general direction he was headed; while still-hunting the thick cover, you come to an opening where you can glass 250 yards across the canyon at some country that can't be seen from anywhere else on the mountain and BAM! There stands a great buck, head down, with 20 yards to go before he's hidden … you rest your rifle in the crotch of two branches and pull in a breath.

That, my friend, is how it happens in real life in real deer country for the complete deer hunter.

In closing, to become a successful big buck hunter, you must learn when and where to apply the techniques, when to switch from one to the other, and when to apply several at once. This ability can come only with practice. In the world of trainers and athletes, we use the term *automaticity* to describe the ability to complete a task without occupying the mind with the low-level details required. Completion of the task becomes an automatic response or habit for the person who's developed their skill to point of automaticity. For you to become an excellent big buck hunter, you must learn, repeat, and practice the techniques I've laid out. In time, you'll be able to do this naturally with little thought, just as a world-class athlete does in his sport.

It took me 35 years to learn enough about big mule deer to write this book. I had to get beyond optics to become successful at killing big mule deer in all the places and ways that they live. My hope is that I've written a book that helps you become a complete mule deer hunter. By applying all the techniques I've detailed here, only you can decide if I've successfully accomplished that.

I've also completely enjoyed a thousand days in mule deer country … and I've asked God for a thousand more. I hope you get to enjoy the same.

I killed this heavy Colorado buck in an area mixed with open country and heavy cover. Even though the range was 300 yards, I killed him in a small opening in the piñon-juniper cover by obeying the wind, still-hunting, tracking, and glassing.

If you'd like to join me on a mule deer hunt, make sure you stop in to Rokslide.com and find my blog. I host several live deer hunts there each fall where I post video, pictures, and text live from the field. You'll see many of these techniques in action and occasionally I tip over a big buck on these hunts. It's not the Outdoor Channel, but I guarantee you'll learn a thing or two. Or you could consider booking a hunt for mule deer through my outfitting service, WeScout4u.com – it's not cheap and openings book quickly, so don't delay if you're serious. May God bless your deer hunting and your life.

~ Robby Denning

The End.

STUFF FOR CHRISTIANS AND THOSE SO INCLINED

Stacy Beazer-Rogers

T HE MENTIONS OF GOD'S NAME IN THIS BOOK are not words lightly written. He's given me the life I enjoy and all the good I've seen has come from Him. I wanted to include a chapter to encourage my fellow brothers and sisters in the LORD and invite anyone with a curiosity about God to explore the possibilities of a life lived in Him.

First, the title of this chapter is really a disclaimer or a warning of sorts. If you're "offended" by the religion of the Bible, then you might want to close this book now. After all, you came here to be a better deer hunter and not listen to a sermon – I understand that. However, before you move on, I want you to know that the only "religion" I find in the Bible is caring for widows and orphans. How anyone could be offended by that is beyond me. I find what really offends most men is that the Bible calls for an allegiance and dependence on God. This notion flies in the face of the manly men who want to depend only on themselves – that is, until they're in need of a diaper change on their deathbed or see the semi-truck in the oncoming lane, then dependence on God isn't so unmanly. So, if you're completely happy and satisfied with your life now, then the rest of this chapter will be meaningless and I take no offense if you choose not to read it.

I decided to follow the Jesus of the Bible when I was 23 years old. It was the best decision I've ever made. My life changed almost immediately.

While I struggled (still do) to follow the path that an allegiance to God requires, I saw His blessing begin to flow upon my then-tumultuous life. Had I not chosen to give my life to Him, this book would have never have happened. Oh no, I'd probably still be trying to sort out my chaotic life of being financially destitute and married four or five times with little kids strewn about. That was the life I was heading for without the LORD. Book? Ha ha ha. Buck Hunting? Forget about it! Happy fulfilling marriage with great kids? Not a chance. Yet it all has happened by following the LORD and I was able to discover *one* of the things I was meant to do: hunt mule deer.

If you're a Christian, you have the most incredible gift ever given to man: peace with God and the promise of a better life both here and after you die. When I'm at my worst, I'm not believing in His goodness and His love for me. When I'm at my best, I'm walking closely with Him believing He will do good in me and through me.

I want to encourage you to seize the gift you've been given and exercise your faith in Him. If there is a God, there is a devil who seeks to destroy your life:

> "The thief does not come except to steal, and to kill, and to destroy. I have come that they may have life, and that they may have *it* more abundantly." John 10:10 (NKJV).

To experience this abundant life, you have to choose daily to follow God. Find a quiet time to read His word in the Bible daily, make sure you're in a good Bible-believing church every week, and exercise your faith through doing good. He'll take care of the rest:

> "But more than anything else, put God's work first and do what He wants. Then the other things will be yours as well," Matthew 6:33 (CEV)

I've put these verses and all of God's word into practice as best as I can. I can tell you that He keeps His promises.

If you're one of the lucky men who get to be a father, consider it one of your highest callings to lead those children in the ways of the LORD. Look around at the disintegration of our society. If you're paying attention, you can see many of our woes are caused by fathers not leading their families. While I'm a struggling sinner saved only by the grace of God, I choose daily to lead my family as best as I can. Although I fall often, I always get back up, dust myself off, take my wife's hand, and step out again. I encourage you to do the same. Remember, His promise and warning in Malachi 4:6:

"And He will turn the hearts of the fathers to the children,
And the hearts of the children to their fathers,
Lest I come and strike the earth with a curse." (NKJV)

Fellow fathers, this is our job. I can promise that if you'll follow as He leads, He will bless you and yours abundantly, in ways you can't even imagine. I've seen it firsthand.

If you're not a father, look around. There are many kids who need your presence in their lives and there is hardly a better place to spend time with them than in God's great outdoors. If you're available to help and lead our next generation, please check out www.fathersinthefield.com founded by John Smithbaker, former CEO of Brunton Optics.

If you're not a Christian and have read this far, maybe you should give His ways a try. First you must agree you've broken His laws. Grab a Bible and look up the Ten Commandments in Exodus chapter 20 (watch out for number 9). If you agree that you've broken any one of those commandments, then God's hand is extended to you in forgiveness, but you need to act. The true message of the Bible is that God sent his perfect sinless son, Jesus, to pay the penalty of death for your breach of those commandments – "sin" as it's called in the Bible. All you have to do is believe that Jesus died for you and turn and follow Him. You will be at peace with God now and forever. It's that simple, no matter what you've heard or think. I choose to be forgiven and to follow. I encourage you to do the same and discover the life He has for you.

> "Oh, taste and see that the LORD is good; Blessed is the man who trusts Him!" Psalm 34:8 (NKJV)

GEAR LIST

This is the main list I use before any backcountry hunt. I don't bring every piece of gear on every hunt. If I'm going to be staying in a road camp, I may add propane heaters, a boot dryer, five-gallon water jugs, and a folding table.

Tack/Horses

Riding saddle

Pack saddle

Rope cinch

Headstalls with bit

Lead ropes

Panniers

Hobble with picket line

Grain

Bug spray

Brush

Tarp

Horse first aid

Hay/Cube

Coggins / health inspection

Camp

Tent

Stakes

Sleeping pad

Sleeping bag

Pillow

Cot

Tarp(s)

Cookstove

Pots/griddle

Silverware

Lighter

Paper Towels

Toilet Paper

Chair

White Gas

Propane

First Aid

Pack Frame

Water Bottles

Water Filter

Gun

Ammo

Gun cleaning kit

Knives

Radio

Camera

Film/Batteries

Army parka

Game bags

Batteries

Flashlight

Rope

Wood/Screws for Table

Pen/Paper/Journal

Mousetrap

Food

Get food out of fridge/freezer before leaving

Ice	Coffee
Gorp	Onion
P&J or honey sandwiches	Garlic
Oatmeal/GrapeNuts	Stuffing
Powdered milk	Ketchup
Meat	Hot Wings
Fish	Mashed Potatoes
Mac & Cheese	Gravy
Microwave Meals	Crystal Light/Tang
Margarine	Brown Sugar
Side Dishes	Salt & Pepper
Spaghetti and olive oil	Water
Microwave Rice	

Clothes

Light wool pants	Pacs with removable liner
Cotton pants	Gators
Weatherproof wool pants	Belt
Light wool shirt	Gloves light
Puffy	Gloves heavy
Wool socks	Gloves work
Long johns top & bottom	Rain gear
Briefs	Hat/headband/neck gaiter
Light boots	Hunter Orange

Backpack

Binoculars/rangefinder	Lip balm
15X Binoculars	SPOT
Spotting Scope	Cell Phone
Tripod	Space Blanket
Fire starter	Firestarter pack (shirt pocket)
Rope	GPS
Knife/sharpener	Reading Glasses
Flashlight	License/tag

CPSIA information can be obtained
at www.ICGtesting.com
Printed in the USA
BVHW090717011118
531456BV00001B/3/P